Goodbye, Arkadelphia!

Goodbye, Arkadelphia!

Turning Obstacles Into Opportunities

by Robert L. Harris

About the Author

At an early age, Robert Lewis Harris was convinced by his parents, who never graduated from high school, that education is liberation that can never be chained. His early days in a dilapidated Jim Crow two-room rural elementary school inspired him to dream beyond the hot cotton fields of Arkadelphia, Arkansas, where his Black teachers inspired confidence in him that one day he would shed the shackles of segregation.

Goodbye, Arkadelphia! tells the story of Robert's exciting and inspirational journey from Arkadelphia to an executive suite in a Fortune 500 Company in San Francisco. As an attorney for the Pacific Gas and Electric Company (PG&E), he became the first—and still the only—Black attorney in the nation to argue (and win) a corporate First Amendment case before the U.S. Supreme Court.

Library of Congress Cataloging-in-Publication Data
Harris, Robert L., 1944–
Goodbye, Arkadelphia! Turning Obstacles Into Opportunities

ISBN:	Hardcover	978-1-5136-2116-6
	Softcover	978-1-5136-2117-3
	Ebook	978-1-5136-2118-0

This book was printed in the United States of America.

To order additional copies of this book, contact:
RLH44@yahoo.com
(415) 850-6432

Dedication

To my parents, Lucy Lois Luster Harris and Benjamin Franklin Harris, for insisting that I work hard and pursue an education; and my wife, Glenda Felicia Newell-Harris, for her love and tenacious support.

Table of Contents

Acknowledgments

For their encouragement and support, I want to thank my siblings and their spouses: Wilma Jean Harris and Artis Blacksher; Leonard Franklin Harris and Sedonia Harris; Harold James Harris and Angela Harris; and Charles Cornelius Harris and Jimie Harris.

For their devotion and dedication, I extend my love to my children and their spouses: Anthony Lester Harris and Rochelle Hackley Harris; Regina Carol Harris and Jerard Nau; Brittany Virginia Lucille Harris; and Phillip Lewis Newell Harris.

For their admiration and inspiration, I want to praise my grandchildren: Ariel Harris, Brianna Harris, Joseph Harrison McNeal, Romeo Maximus McNeal, Nia Nau, and Anthony Elijah Harris.

For their loyalty and patience, I extend my gratitude to all my colleagues and friends over my lifetime.

For helping me to launch this project by asking probing questions, suggesting an outline, and transcribing the recordings I made, I extend special thanks to Ariel Jolicoeur.

For organizing, editing, and making sense of the voluminous materials I used to write this book, I am extremely grateful to Dorothy Reed.

For his final editorial polish of my manuscript, I deeply appreciate the expertise of Paul Weisser.

1

A Long Way from Arkadelphia

We are prone to judge success by the index of our salaries or the size of our automobiles, rather than by the quality of our service and relationship to humanity.

—Martin Luther King, Jr.

When Dr. Martin Luther King, Jr., was assassinated in Memphis, Tennessee, on April 4, 1968, I was a twenty-four-year-old deputy probation officer with the Alameda County Probation Department in Oakland, California. I had been on the job for almost three years after graduating from college. With about eighty juveniles under my careful supervision, I had been quite content with my chosen profession, believing that I was making a game-changing difference in helping mildly delinquent boys, most of whom were African American, to avoid incarceration. The money was good, supporting my family and paying my bills, but a single shot from a Remington rifle aimed at Dr. King on the second-floor balcony of the Lorraine Motel changed the course of my life.

The day before his assassination, Dr. King, as if he could see what was coming, concluded a speech with the following prescient words:

> Like anybody, I would like to live a long life. Longevity has its place. But I'm not concerned about that now. I just want to do God's will. And He's allowed me to go up to the mountain. And I've looked over. And I've seen the Promised Land. I may not get there with you. But I want you to know tonight that we, as a people, will get to the promised land!

I think Dr. King believed that his efforts would bear fruit, no matter what—a hope that failed many of us in the wake of his assassination. But Dr. King was right, and I am living proof. It was the fatal shooting of the Nobel Peace prize–winning civil rights leader that led the University of California Berkeley School of Law, known then as Boalt Hall, which consistently has ranked among the top law schools in the country, to make its first concerted effort to open its doors to more Black students. Prior to that, the law school had admitted one, two, or three Black students into each class.

Now, I had never really given much, if any, thought to attending law school, but when I got word from a White colleague at the Probation Department that Boalt Hall was looking for candidates who looked like me, I applied and was accepted into the Class of 1972.

Was I prepared? Well, apparently so—although, believe me, I didn't know it at first. Yet, I would distinguish myself by being elected to the Law Review, for which I published two articles. I would go on to succeed in my legal career, even arguing a landmark case before the United States Supreme

Court. And I would ultimately become a vice president of a Fortune 500 company.

How did I do it? That is what I contemplate now in retirement. I think it is fair to say that my success was against the odds. I had received my primary education in a segregated two-room schoolhouse in rural Arkansas, where I used hand-me-down textbooks from the White schools. All but one year of my secondary education was spent in a segregated under-financed high school in the small city of Arkadelphia (population at that time, approximately 7,000). And throughout those years, my early classroom education was possible only when I wasn't out in the fields picking cotton.

I can still taste that devilish sweat of hard physical labor in the fields, with my father preaching, "God helps those who help themselves." That got me through the morning.

And I can still smell my mother's heavenly peach cobbler. Oh, what a delight! That got me through the evening.

Often, though, reflecting on my past can be unsettling, perhaps because I lived in such a different world back then from the privileged one I live in today. Now I belong to an exclusive golf course, drive a Mercedes Benz, and fly first-class on airplanes all over the world. I've come a long way from Arkadelphia.

At the same time, however, I see a flashback of a different me—the determination on the face of the little boy that I was in the back of the truck heading to the cotton fields.

That was my early reality. I didn't know I was poor, but I knew I didn't have a whole lot, I had to work hard for everything I got, and I had to make the most of everything I had. And I did.

2

Cotton Pickers

Still I Rise

Out of the huts of history's shame
I rise
Up from a past that's rooted in pain
I rise
I'm a Black ocean, leaping and wide,
Welling and swelling I bear in the tide.

Leaving behind nights of terror and fear
I rise
Into a daybreak that's wondrously clear
I rise
Bringing the gifts that my ancestors gave,
I am the dream and the hope of the slave.
I rise
I rise
I rise.

— Maya Angelou

For over three generations, cotton had been essential to the livelihood of my people, the Harris clan. When I was born in 1944, rural Arkadelphia was a sweltering swath of cotton fields—literally a sun-powered open oven.

This is what little I know about my Harris ancestors and how they came to settle in Arkansas. My great-grandfather, James Harris, the illegitimate son of a White slavemaster, was born in Wake Forest, North Carolina, in August 1842. I don't even know his mother's name. James's son, my grandfather, Henry H. Harris, also born in Wake Forest, in September 1879, was James's seventh child with his wife, Ailey.

Henry was about ten years old when the family took a shot at improving their lives by migrating from North Carolina to Arkansas, which was considered a cotton-growing land of opportunity at the time. After traveling more than eight hundred miles—whether on foot or in a covered wagon, I don't know—they settled in a place called Manchester.

Manchester is eleven miles outside the city limits of Arkadelphia, in the southwestern region of the state, about a hundred miles from the Texas border. It was country then, and it still is today. The nearest place of historical note—some forty-eight miles away—is Hope, Arkansas, the childhood home of the forty-second president of the United States, William Jefferson Clinton.

In 1901, Henry Harris, my grandfather, married Mary Williams, the daughter of Shandy Williams, a Black farmer, and his wife, Liza Jones. At one point, Grandpa Harris owned over a hundred acres, mostly devoted to growing cotton. All of his twelve children worked in the fields, including the youngest son, my father, Benjamin Franklin Harris. Although no one ever said so, I suspect that my grandfather named his son after the Founding Father because, like him, he firmly believed that "a penny saved is a penny earned." And my father, too, believed in Franklin's proverb as much as he believed in grace—once it amazed him.

My Grandparents, Henry and Mary Williams Harris

Ben, as he was called, was born on May 10, 1918, in Manchester. He attended the segregated two-room Williams Elementary School, the same grammar school I would later attend. After completing tenth grade at the segregated Peake High School in Arkadelphia, he dropped out to work full-time, picking cotton and helping with other farm chores.

Daddy was slightly built, standing no more than five-feet-seven, but he was all rock-solid muscle and proudly proved to be an extremely productive worker all his life. He was a good-looking boy, or at least he thought he was. And before he was "saved and sanctified" in the Church of God in Christ, I'm told he loved to dance to the popular music of his day, jazz, the so-called devil's music. He was also a bit of a ladies' man.

Daddy's romancing days ended in 1939, when he married Lucy Lois Luster, my mother, following a year of courtship. Lucy was a seventeen-year-old beauty with a contagious sense of humor, who could sing so well that she took church out of church and brought it home as she washed dishes or did some other mundane chore. She was the granddaughter of a slave, Danny "Babe" Luster, whose roots in the Manchester area date back to the 1860s.

Danny married Gracie Macon, but we don't know where she came from. What we do know is that she had a dozen children. Lucy, my mother, who was born on Christmas Day, 1922, was the second youngest of her siblings. She attended school at the segregated Piney Grove Elementary School through third grade before having to drop out to assist with home chores after the death of her mother, possibly from cancer. No one knows for sure. My mother rarely spoke of it.

Lucy could read and write, but was a housewife, housekeeper, and domestic worker throughout her life. If she had had unlimited educational opportunities, she could have entered any profession of her choosing and been a success, because she was, in a word, brilliant. She had an encyclopedic memory and, even in later years, could recall the tiniest details of largely forgotten events that had taken place fifty years or more earlier.

Daddy, too, was brilliant. He was notably gifted with a good head for numbers, as old folks would say. In other words, he computed nearly as fast as a calculator and forgot none of it. He would have made a great engineer or doctor. In fact, he would have excelled in whatever profession he chose.

I am blessed to have had such parents.

Ben and Lucy exchanged vows in a simple ceremony at the Arkadelphia Courthouse, attended by family and a few close friends, as was the Black custom in those days. Two years later, they purchased twenty acres and a small house from my paternal grandfather, Henry, for five hundred dollars. The down payment was a horse valued at one hundred dollars. Ben and Lucy raised five children on those twenty acres, and all of us picked cotton, although some of us were more productive than others.

Their first child was born on February 27, 1940. Wilma Jean, the only girl they would have, was a beauty with rich brown coloring close to Mother's. I guess that since she was the oldest, she was instructed to be (and properly considered herself) the boss and protector of her younger brothers. And that she was, both in and out of the cotton fields. Jean was short (five-feet-three)—but then, remember, dynamite comes in small packages.

Leonard, born fourteen months after Jean (April 11, 1941), was also small in stature (five-feet-four), but it was nearly impossible to outwork him. "Shorty," as he was sometimes called, could readily pick three hundred pounds of cotton per day, easily competing with others twice his size. A short stature didn't diminish him one bit.

As the middle child, born on March 4, 1944, I willingly took directions from Jean and dutifully followed the example of Leonard. Although I could easily do my fair share of work, I was no match for my "big" brother, but I did grow taller than him by four inches. Thankfully, I also distinguished myself in another way, when Mother enrolled precocious little me in the first grade at age five. We didn't have kindergarten back then, but she believed that I would soar nonetheless. (Family lore has it that I entered first grade at age four, a compliment I never questioned, but I've done the math: I was five.)

Where I Was Born

Sixteen months my junior, Harold, the fourth sibling, was born on July 26, 1946. From the very beginning, Harold sang a different tune than the rest of us, for he was not noted for his working skills. Picking cotton was simply not his gift or desire, and no amount of discipline could change that. Mother and Daddy had to resign themselves to the fact that if Harold picked 150 pounds of cotton, that was a huge stretch over his average of 100 pounds per day. At that time, I was picking between 200 and 300 pounds of cotton per day.

Charles, the baby of the family, arrived five years after Harold, on March 2, 1951. By the time he was ten, which was considered an excellent age to pick cotton, the industry was beginning to fall prey to new technology in the form of cotton-picking machines. Like me, "Charlie," as we always called him then, was considered to be very smart. Eventually, he became an engineer with a Fortune 500 company after receiving his undergraduate and graduate degrees in civil engineering from

Stanford.

I still sweat as I think back to age six, when I toiled in those sizzling cotton fields from sunup to sundown with little relief. By then, Daddy was working at a brickyard thirty miles away in Malvern, but everybody else—Mother and the first four of us—was expected to pick cotton daily during the season in order to earn additional funds to buy needed supplies.

Unlike chopping (or thinning out) cotton, which took place in the spring of the year and necessitated certain skills that usually required one to be at least eight or nine years old, picking cotton only required the ability to pull the cotton out of the boll. However, picking 200 to 300 pounds of cotton was more of a science than an art. Adopting the right cotton-picking style made a lot of difference, and one style did not fit all. Some folks preferred picking two cotton rows at a time, while others preferred straddling one row. My own preference was to pick two rows at a time.

In the 1950s, cotton was a profitable enterprise for the owners, who received around thirty-three cents per pound. However, the cotton pickers were paid only about three cents per pound. But if you were an outstanding picker, it was possible to earn as much as ten dollars a day or more. For example, 100 pounds of cotton would earn you three dollars. But picking only 100 pounds per day was considered poor performance. The average per day was 200 pounds, with high performance being 300 pounds or more, which could earn one almost ten dollars per day—"good money" in the 1950s. Both my mother and Jean were in the average range, but occasionally Jean, despite her small stature, would reach the 300-pound level, especially when she got to her early teens.

One fringe benefit of picking cotton all week was the opportunity to travel on Saturday afternoons to Arkadelphia—or "town," as we called it. That didn't happen every week, but occasionally, after picking cotton all Saturday morning, we were rewarded with the privilege of going to town around noon in a loaded truck that was headed to the cotton gin. I can still remember how we all sat perched on top of the tightly packed cargo as we crossed the Ouachita River, the demarcation between townspeople and country folk.

Just seeing several stores in town, which appeared to be huge, was a treat, especially when we were allowed to buy candy and ice cream. Back in Manchester, we had a small store about a mile from our home. It was one room of a white man's house that he called Hardeman's Grocery Store. Mother sent us there sometimes for items like bread, which I can recall cost a nickel a loaf.

Since racial segregation was strictly enforced, we had been cautioned to obey all the laws in town, such as drinking only from water fountains marked "Colored Only," and staying away from fountains marked "Whites Only." The same applied to the movie theater, which relegated Blacks to the balcony. Every aspect of town was rigidly segregated, and we had been cautioned not to "talk back" to White people.

For me that was curious, but I never thought about defying the status quo. I was merely a young boy experiencing the excitement of seeing things I never saw back "across the river." Just to drink out of a water fountain was a luxury, and to use indoor bathrooms rather than outhouses—even if they *were* "Colored only"—was something really special.

One of those Saturday afternoons in town gave me my first

opportunity to go to a "picture show," as movies were called in the early 1950s. Cowboys and Indians fought it out on a huge screen, which was a singular experience that didn't compare to anything I had ever seen. I sat awestruck in the colored section upstairs, undistracted in the least by thoughts like *Why do I have to sit up here?* I knew why. White folks didn't want to mix with colored people, but that didn't diminish the thrill of the movie one bit. It was clear to me from a young age that White people thought they were superior to us, but it probably didn't lower my self-esteem, because I never believed that.

The cotton-picking season started in late August and usually lasted through the middle of October. We mostly worked for White farmers, Clarence Daniel and his brothers, who would pick us up in a truck at 5:30 in the morning. There was nothing romantic about the cotton fields. They were boiling hot and suffocatingly humid, and the work could be brutal to the knees, the back, and the hands. Moreover, it was not unusual to encounter snakes enjoying the sun out in the fields, but it was rare that the snakes posed a serious danger—because, for the most part, we didn't bother them, and they didn't bother us.

To me, the only good snake was a dead snake. My mother was afraid of snakes and passed that fear on to her children. She would always remind us when we were picking cotton, playing, or just walking down dusty dirt roads to look out for snakes.

"Be aware of them," she used to say. "They see you when you don't see them, and if you can see them or know they're around, you can protect yourself from them."

I will never forget her admonition that "if you don't know they're there, then you can get bitten."

I recall one summer night during church services, while some of us were outside making mischief when we should have been in church, I saw what a snake can do. My friend Elijah Brim and I were playing with some other kids in a poorly lit space between the church and the school, close to a water pump, when, all of a sudden, I heard a rattling sound. But before I even realized what it was, Elijah cried out in pain.

The alarmed adults rushed out with flashlights and lanterns. A short distance from the pump, someone spotted a rattlesnake and immediately killed it with a stick. Then Elijah was rushed to a White doctor in Arkadelphia (I never saw a Black doctor until I moved to California), and was treated successfully. Luckily for him, the snake was not fully grown, which explained why its venom was not lethal.

For me, it was a sage reminder of the necessity to always be on the lookout for rattlesnakes. You may never know where they are until they strike! And it's one of those lessons that influenced critical decisions I would make as an adult.

An even greater threat than snakes was the burning hot sun, particularly in midday. I remember my Aunt Maggie working one day in the early afternoon when the temperature was almost 100 degrees. She was singing an old "Negro" spiritual as she struggled with an 8-foot-long cotton sack over her shoulder, bending over the cotton row and picking to the rhythm of her song. Suddenly, she stood straight up, wiped the sweat from her forehead, and collapsed. I saw her as she fell to the ground. Immediately, someone rushed to assist her to the nearest tree, about five hundred yards away, where she was given cool water.

Between the heat and the snakes, I learned how important

it is to figure out the conditions under which you work. You have to know your environment and adapt to it. Stay hydrated. Watch out for snakes. Pace yourself.

At 6:00 in the morning, because the dew was plentiful, the cotton was quite wet and thus very heavy. By starting early in the morning, it was not unusual for a high-performing cotton picker to gather two hundred pounds by noon. Once the heat of the day—95 to 100 degrees—baked the cotton, it became almost as light as a feather, so regardless of how much cotton was packed in the sack, it was still going to weigh very little, which spoke to the wisdom of early morning picking.

While my family expected everyone to work hard, with each person carrying his or her own weight, there was also a firm emphasis on education, which to some extent seemed contradictory to me as a child. My mother and father would often say to me and my siblings, "Get an education, because it's something nobody can take from you."

But at the beginning of every school year, we were forced to miss several weeks. I remember once saying to my parents, "If getting an education is so important, then why do I have to stay out of school to pick cotton?" Obviously, I was trying to get out of picking cotton.

Their response was that it was also necessary to learn how to work and assist in paying for our clothes to attend school. When I would ask why that should be the case, they would always respond, "You're a very smart boy..., so smart that you can catch up with your classmates when you finish picking cotton."

The lesson my parents were teaching me was that even if I had to sacrifice my attendance at the beginning of the school year, I could still be competitive if I were willing to work harder than my classmates. I learned that there's something very valuable about competition. It can force you to outperform yourself. This became a foundational belief that has guided me throughout the years.

Hard work. I also heard about that from my grandfather, Henry Harris, who firmly believed that an idle mind was the "devil's workshop." Our parents, who were more liberal than Grandpa, allowed us to do a fair amount of playing when we weren't working in the fields or doing other chores. But it almost made Grandpa sick to see us not working. He lived in a house down the road from us and would frequently make visits to our home. I'll always remember the day when he suddenly appeared, seemingly out of nowhere, as we were playing in the yard. Startled by his unannounced presence, we stopped, and he commenced to sternly lecture us on the ethics of work over play.

"Kids," he said, "you ought to be ashamed of yourselves, wasting time playing when you could be working."

Without thinking, I said, "Grandpa, we don't have any work to do!"

He glanced at me for a long time and then sternly responded, "Son, there's *always* work to do. Do you see that rock over there? Go and get it and move it over here."

I did.

Then, pointing to a different area of the yard, he said, "Now take that rock over to the other corner of the yard."

We quickly got the message that he really believed that even makeshift work is better than wasting time.

So, we adapted. Our problem with Grandpa was solved

by all of us keeping a keen eye out for him so that we could pretend to work whenever he made his unannounced visits. We became quite skilled at outfoxing him, but his admonitions did not fall on deaf ears. While he never really convinced us that we should work for the sake of working, particularly when there was free time and fun to be had, he did reinforce what our parents were trying to teach us—that hard work builds character and creates opportunities. Lazy people often miss that lesson because they fail to understand that work can be energizing and stimulating to the imagination, the source of all invention. Probably most of our tools have been invented by someone hard at work, asking the question, "Isn't there a simpler or better way to do this?"

For us children, country life provided ample opportunities to practice these virtues because we did a lot more than picking cotton. For one, we also had an extensive garden. Whether planting collard greens, cabbage, black-eyed peas, purple hull peas, turnip greens, string beans, or watermelons—to name a few of the items raised in our garden—we all participated.

Our contributions depended on our ability to deal with farm animals, which required unique skills, testing our courage and fortitude. But it could also be fun. Chickens, cows, and pigs were the key animals we raised. We also had a mule and several horses to hitch to the plows to till the soil. By the age of eight, I could handle that job quite well, plowing at least an acre of land in three hours without difficulty.

Plowing required keen observation, the right communication with the animals, and good timing. When hitched to the plows, the horses had on a harness that allowed them to be guided correctly as the soil was tilled. Two words were used to communicate with them. *Gee!* told them to move to the right, and *Haw!* told them to move to the left. Sometimes it seemed that the horses were constantly shuffling from left to right in order to make the plow go in a straight line, but it worked, guaranteeing that the soil was plowed correctly.

Alternatively, the horses could be guided manually rather than verbally by pulling the lines attached to the harness. To me, the verbal communications were more interactive and expressive. You had to say the words in just the right tone and volume and at precisely the right moment.

The most exciting aspect of owning horses was the opportunity to ride them, with or without a saddle. My horse riding was done bareback and often not for pleasure, but as a means of viable transportation, particularly when the distance exceeded a mile. It was also not unusual to hitch a couple of horses to a wagon for transportation when we had to haul hay or other items in large quantities, especially to areas where cars couldn't go.

The cows provided milk and were often slaughtered for beef. Early in life, I learned how to milk them. From our cows' milk, we made three products: whole milk, butter, and buttermilk. Butter was the byproduct of churning the whole milk to make the buttermilk. Actually, it was a fairly sophisticated process.

The phrase *slopping the pigs* meant feeding the pigs, which was something we often did with our leftover food. We had a hog pen, where we raised at least three or four cute little piglets for the purpose of growing them into big fat hogs. It was important to slop each day, giving them as much food as they could possibly eat, and then some. I suppose the phrase *eating like a pig* came from this concept of overfeeding the pigs to get them ready for slaughter after they had grown into hogs to be consumed as winter food.

For me, hog killing time came with mixed emotions. Having spent several long months nourishing a couple of cute little piglets into big fat hogs, I found it difficult to say goodbye. Slaughtering them seemed so cruel, but that sadness was only momentary as images of bacon, ham, ribs, and sausages invaded my mind. The killing of the hogs, which was carried out by Daddy and some of his friends in a variety of ways, was unpleasant for me to witness. Once the process was over and the elaborate preparation of the hog for carving was completed, the task of portioning the animal into various segments was begun. In addition to the bacon, ham, and other parts, the hog was also the source of chitterlings, pig's feet, pig's tails, hog jowls, ham hocks, and, yes, hog's brains. Considered a delicacy because of their resemblance to scrambled eggs, the brains were highly prized.

The bacon, ham, and sausages were "cured" with salt so they could be put into a "smokehouse" to be eaten during the winter months. Because of the value of that meat, it was important to have a lock on the smokehouse, because otherwise someone might "liberate" the meat. It wasn't a big problem, but it was a problem. Pork was king in the country.

Every part of the hog was used for eating, which made it a valuable asset for families with lots of mouths to feed. Absolutely nothing was wasted. Going hungry in the country was a foreign concept because of the ingenuity of what my adult corporate mind would call "asset utilization." Hogs were evidence of asset utilization taken to the extreme—something we did wisely and proudly. In the final analysis, it mattered not what assets we had; rather, it mattered most what we *did* with what we had.

While utilizing every aspect of our hogs was a way of life for us, so too was the wise utilization of other food items. Not having food to eat was never a concern, but having the option of saying we didn't like certain foods was not available if we were actually hungry. Oftentimes, on Daddy's way home from work, he stopped at the store for food items we didn't produce ourselves. At home, he would carefully note the foods we claimed not to like—say, some kind of syrup—and then he would buy precisely *that* the next time. We ate what was put before us.

Farming wasn't all hard work, the kind that made your muscles burn at night. There was a lot of fun to be had, too—the mischievous kind that little boys can't resist. Looking back, I can still see with mouth-watering delight the patches where huge watermelons weighing up to sixty pounds were grown. Liberating one or more of those humongous fruits without getting caught was a big deal. Just about every family had a watermelon patch, some better than others.

My great-uncle, Jacob Williams, was noted for having the best watermelons around. Often a whole group of us boys would get together to test our skills at raiding his patch. It was not that we were stealing the watermelons for money; rather, we were doing it for thrills. Our satisfaction came from successfully invading the patch and swiping two or more melons, bursting them open, and eating the "heart," which was the big red part of the inner section of the melon that tasted exceptionally delicious, cool, and watery just when you needed it. For us, it was worth the risk of getting caught. And, fortunately, we never did. I'd like to think we got away with it, but then maybe Uncle Jacob was watching us from a discreet distance, smiling as only a grown man with a little boy's heart can do.

3

Nothing Like Family

This is no mountain
But a house,
No rock of solitude
But a family chair,
No wilds
But life appearing
As life anywhere domesticated,
Yet I know the gods are here,
And that if I touch them
I will arise
And take majesty into the kitchen.

—Jean Toomer

Our family home was originally a one-story, four-room house, about four hundred square feet, situated on a dirt road with no street signs. It was well off the main road, and its driveway—instead of neatly trimmed hedges, concrete pillars, or marble lions—was marked by two discarded car tires. During the rainy winter season, the house could only be reached by precarious driving or wading on foot through thick mud.

We lived way back in the woods—so far back that they had to pump air into us. When I see the house as it appears in my earliest memories, I see two large oak trees in the front yard that were planted sometime in the 1930s, before I was born, by Uncle Robert Harris, after whom I am named. Pillars of nature they were, and protective sun blockers in the sweaty season. I can still hear the sound of driving raindrops falling on the tin roof of our house. When the rain came down hard, the roof often leaked, but the tap-tap-tapping as it intensified was melodious to my young ears.

This was our land of opportunity and our home.

Initially, the whitewashed wooden house consisted of a kitchen, a living room, and two small bedrooms with a front porch. There was no running water, only well water drawn with a bucket in the backyard. In the late 1940s, when I was five years old, electricity came to my community. Prior to that, we had candles and kerosene lamps.

Mother said, "We've come out of the darkness into the light."

Mother, Me (at 2), Leonard, and Harold (clockwise)

Electricity really changed our lives. Now there was radio and with it music, entertainment, sports, and information from faraway places. In 1950, Daddy gave up the "ice box" and purchased a refrigerator with a freezer compartment, and Mother made us popsicles and ice cream. What more could a kid in the country possibly want on a brutally hot summer day?

Everything seemed to be on the move for the family with the introduction of electricity. Without Daddy's knowledge or consent, Mother saved enough money from our cotton-picking earnings to purchase a television set. One day, when Daddy was away, she had it delivered and an antenna installed on the side of the house. When Daddy walked in and saw it, he was shocked and probably a little miffed, but he didn't put up any argument.

"It's for the children," Mother said, and that was it.

Before that TV set came into our house, television had already influenced how I saw the world and how I wanted to see myself in it as I grew up. That's because my great-uncle and great-aunt, Joseph and Snowrene Williams, had already introduced our close-knit community to TV. No longer were we distant subjects across the Ouachita River, isolated from the rest of the world. We now had the rest of the world coming to us in black-and-white.

As was traditional and expected, my relatives opened their doors wide to all the children, giving them the chance to come and watch TV. The hours of viewing were limited to Saturdays. We were eager to see anything, especially the classic westerns of the 1950s like *The Lone Ranger*—but really almost any show that took us out of Manchester. Those were moments to dream and seek refuge in another world divorced from the harsh realities of hard work under a burning hot sun. They gave me hope that if I worked hard, my future might be very different from my present.

My interior and exterior worlds changed significantly in the mid-1950s. Although Daddy was frugal, he was motivated to expand. One time, he consulted with Uncle Jacob Williams (of watermelon fame), his mother's brother, who was a jack-of-all-trades, and they spent several weeks adding two more rooms to our house. I could hardly believe what I was seeing. When completed, a new kitchen and another bedroom had been added. The old kitchen became the dining room. The new bedroom was for my parents. Now Jean had her own bedroom, and the boys were all together in their bedroom.

With all of this change swiftly engulfing us, the fact that we didn't have hot and cold running water or indoor toilet facilities wasn't a big deal. I didn't mind drawing water from the well and using the gas stove in the kitchen to heat the water to fill our number 3 tin tub for my weekly bath. Yet, I was acutely aware of certain challenges posed at night by the lack of an indoor toilet. We had what was known as an outhouse, built a reasonable distance from the house and away from the flow of the underground water so that human waste wouldn't mix with our drinking water.

The outhouse was pretty basic: a hole in the ground over which a small wooden shed was constructed. If the urge to use the outhouse after sundown became a necessity, we had to seriously think about the possibility of encountering snakes or other unfriendly creatures as we navigated in the darkness with only a porch light to provide dim guidance. To avoid the challenges of the outhouse at night, we tried as best we could to control the necessity for such visits, but for the most part the partial remedy for the outhouse dilemma was the use of a chamber pot, or slop jar, that could be emptied the next morning into the outhouse. (When I migrated to California in 1960, our outhouse was still in use, and it was not until 1962 that a bathroom was eventually installed.)

Although we didn't have a washing machine, we were never dirty. Mother wouldn't have that. Washing clothes and getting them really clean was more than a notion, but Mother (with the help of my sister) had mastered the skills. With the expert use of a "wash pot" a fire, a bar of soap, and a washboard, she worked miracles on our garments. A clothes dryer was not even in our vocabulary, but a clothesline and abundant sunshine most of the year served us well.

It was in the mid-1950s that the telephone found its way to Manchester. Now, talk about a celebration. For several years in the early 1950s, there was a lot of talk about bringing the telephone to Manchester, but the difficulty was that the telephone company required that a certain number of subscribers had to sign up to bear the cost of installing the necessary poles and wires in that rural area. But finally, enough people signed up, and I remember I could hardly wait to see what it would be like to have a telephone on which I could talk to people I couldn't see. That was a big deal.

The phone system was set up with party lines, which meant that five or six families would share a single line. If one household were on the line, then all the others had to wait. That was a problem for some, but usually people would yield if you claimed an urgent need. However, the fringe benefit of a party line was the ability to listen in on the conversations of other people. For us kids, it was difficult to resist the temptation of easing the phone off the hook to see if you could hear some really juicy gossip, even though we had been warned against eavesdropping.

One day, when I thought Mother was outside in the yard, I decided to do it. When I picked up the phone, sure enough someone was talking. I immediately recognized the voice of my Aunt Flossie Williams, who was deep in a conversation about another woman in Manchester. It was really good gossip! Fully engrossed in listening, I didn't hear Mother coming.

Then all I heard was, "Robert Lewis! What are you doing on that telephone?"

Startled, I blurted out, "I don't know," and gently hung up.

A few minutes later, the phone rang. Mother answered, and it was, as I feared, Aunt Flossie, having put two and two together. My eavesdropping escapade ended abruptly, for the simple reason that the excitement of eavesdropping did not outweigh the punishment for the transgression.

"Go get me a switch," Mother said.

Those were fearsome words to my ears. It meant a whipping was coming, and having to choose the weapon myself, as anyone will tell you, made it hurt that much more.

Although our house met our basic needs, and did improve over time, it was no place to brag about. But it was warm, heated by a wood stove, a propane gas heater, and the loving attention of two parents who adored us. My home was a cheerful one, full of life, mischief, and good food. My most precious memories are of the scents of food cooking, from the sizzling bacon in the morning to the fried chicken in the evening.

In our small world, where almost everyone was related in some way, Mother famously distinguished herself as an outstanding cook—with her hot water cornbread and peach cobblers made with fat fleshy fruit picked at just the ripe moment from our trees in the yard. She made certain that Jean and all of her boys mastered the art of cooking, too.

I recall asking her on one occasion, "Why do we have to learn to cook?"

"Robert Lewis," she said, "I don't want you or the rest of my boys to ever be held hostage to a woman's failure to cook for you."

My cooking skills remain intact to this day.

Mother was effusive with firm hugs and lots of kisses, while Daddy, although seldom displaying affection, provided a sense of security through his focus on hard work and making certain that our basic needs were met. As solid as a rock, he lived by the Bible and firmly believed that "sinners" would end up in Hell. He believed in discipline, but it was Mother who did most of the spanking when we needed it. She was usually persuasive with a switch, although, if necessary, she would use one of Daddy's belts. But her biggest and most effective threat was, "Robert Lewis, you're gonna really get it when Ben comes home."

Mother always referred to Daddy as "Ben," and I knew that when Daddy got home and Mother gave him a vivid description of my bad behavior, I was really going to have to answer to him. It was frightening just to think about it, which actually hurt more than the whipping. Most of Daddy's disciplinary actions were administered with his belt. He didn't just strike; he lectured, too, in a firm voice.

"Robert," he might say, "this is a lesson I have to teach you for doing wrong. It will make you a better person when you grow up."

At that point, I would wonder whether I really wanted to *be* a better person, but he taught me that wrong choices have consequences. It didn't take a genius to figure out whether the behavior was worth the consequences. Thus, I dismissed a lot of things I wanted to do, mostly because of the feared repercussions.

The Ten Commandments were the guiding principles for ideal behavior in my home, but some were taken more seriously than others by me and my siblings. We sometimes found ourselves doing precisely the opposite of what we were taught, including not telling the truth.

Because my parents were regularly off to a church service, but couldn't always take us with them, temptations often presented themselves, enticing us to do things that we thought our parents would never discover. On one occasion, they went to an all-day church service, only taking Charles with them, since he was just a baby. Jean was left in charge, but Mother warned her specifically not to do any cooking. Plenty of food was left for us to eliminate the need to cook, and thus reduce the risk of a fire. But soon after Mother and Daddy left for church, Jean came up with the brilliant idea that even though there were desserts already there for us, she would do something special for us by cooking what in our house we called an egg pie, although some call it egg custard. I have no idea why she came to the conclusion that she knew how to cook such a pie, but she seemed quite excited about doing it, and I certainly liked egg pie. Leonard, too, thought it was a good idea and encouraged her to do it. Harold, who seemed to support everything that appeared to be devious, was quite anxious to have a big slice.

With our support, Jean cheerfully proceeded to prepare what she thought would be an egg pie that would surpass any egg pie that Mother had ever cooked. My brothers and I played outside while she cooked. After perhaps an hour, we began to wonder what had happened to the pie we were eagerly waiting to eat. Then we smelled something burning in the house. When we ran in, we found Jean in the kitchen, standing next to a pie pan, staring at it as if she couldn't believe her eyes.

Leonard, who was the first to get to the kitchen, said, "Jean, what have you burned up? Where's the egg pie?"

By then, Harold and I could see that something had gone seriously wrong.

Never missing an opportunity to tease Jean, Leonard blurted out, "This ain't no egg pie! This is nothing but fried eggs! I told you you didn't know how to cook!"

He began laughing, but Jean was not amused. She knew that her lack of success in making the egg pie now required her to figure out how to keep it a secret from Mother and Daddy. If she had been successful with the pie, there would have been no problem. We all would have had a great time eating the pie. But this "pie" was a disaster, and nobody was happy.

An egg pie is a traditional Southern dish made with eggs as its main ingredient. When it is prepared correctly, it is a yellowish creamy custard that is really delicious. Jean's pie, however, was something even our yard dog wouldn't touch, and we had one of those dogs who devoured nearly every scrap thrown his way. Indeed, Fido would have eaten *himself* to death with his insatiable appetite, had we not apportioned his food.

Jean's pie was awful by any standard. Apparently, she hadn't paid close attention to Mother's cooking of an egg pie, which not only required beaten eggs as the essential ingredient, but also the addition of milk and several other things. Most likely, Jean only prepared the pie crust, beat up some eggs, and poured them into the crust in the pie pan without the other ingredients, especially the milk, and that resulted in the eggs getting fried.

Harold, who loved to eat, was looking forward to having some good old-fashioned egg pie and was quite unhappy that Jean had not delivered on her promise. Within minutes of seeing the mess Jean had created, Harold, being the conniving person he was, looked straight at Jean and said, "I'm gonna tell on you!"

Disappointed and gravely concerned because Mother had specifically instructed her not to cook anything, Jean suddenly realized she had a serious problem on her hands. Especially with Harold constantly repeating, "I'm gonna tell on you!"

Leonard and I weighed in, trying to get Harold not to tell on Jean. After all, she was doing it for us. But Harold insisted he was going to tell on Jean anyway.

Jean threatened to whip him, but quickly changed her mind because that would *certainly* result in him telling on her. Frustrated but knowing Harold, she finally figured out that he actually wanted to be bribed into silence.

So she astutely said to him, "I'll give you fifty cents," which was a lot of money in those days.

Harold readily agreed and collected Jean's hard-earned

savings. Leonard and I thought he was being unfair for taking advantage of the situation, but what could we do? Harold was Harold—out for himself.

With the exception of Jean, who remained in the kitchen to clean up her mess, we all returned to the front yard to play, while keeping a sharp eye on the road to make certain our Grandpa didn't catch us.

By the time our parents returned home from church services, Jean had cleaned the kitchen spotlessly, so the smell of burned egg had long since dissipated from the house. Mother seemed quite pleased.

"You really did a good job in keeping the boys while we were at church," she said to Jean.

But soon after that, Harold just had to say something. Approaching Mother, who was out on the porch, he said, "I ain't gonna tell it."

Mother ignored him, proceeding to chat with us about the church service.

But following Mother as she walked to the other end of the porch, Harold said again, in a slightly louder voice this time, "I ain't gonna tell it!"

Apparently feeling that he was being ignored, he looked straight into Mother's eyes, and said, "I ain't gonna tell it!"

This time, he caught mother's attention. By then Jean had a look of absolute terror on her face. With the third assertion of "I ain't gonna tell it," Mother was starting to look somewhat disconcerted.

"Baby," she said, looking totally puzzled at Harold, "what in the world are you talking about?"

With a huge grin, Harold said, looking Mother in the eyes

for the fourth time, "I ain't gonna tell it!"

Frustrated by his repeated assertions, Mother said, "Harold, what is it that you're not gonna tell me?"

With that, Harold blurted out, "I ain't gonna tell that Jean cooked an egg pie, and the eggs fried in the pie!"

Mother turned to Jean for an explanation. Needless to say, it was not a happy evening for Jean. But neither was it for Harold, because Jean took back the fifty cents she had paid him. We all learned valuable lessons that night. One, what is done in the dark will likely come out in the light. Two, never trust a person who can't keep a secret, even if you pay him to keep quiet. And three, it's better to tell your story before someone else does.

4

Spirit Runs Deep

Gonna lay down my burdens
Down by the riverside
Down by the riverside
Down by the riverside

—Negro spiritual

When not at work, my family was likely in church. On Fridays, Saturdays, and especially Sundays, attending services was like a ritual, and ultimately it was our way of life.

As the story goes, Mother was the first in the family to be saved and converted to the Church of God in Christ. Not long after she married Daddy, she attended a revival one steamy summer night under what was called a tabernacle, a makeshift church built with bushes on top, typical in the country in those days.

The night that Daddy was saved, he may have been consuming a little alcohol. He certainly did not go to the revival with the intention of being saved. He went with the intention of checking on his wife, but when he entered the tabernacle, he felt a force, which he took to be a divine force, propelling him. When he walked up to the altar, he got religion and was saved. Simple as that. Soon after, he was baptized. And soon after that, he got his calling. In those days, you didn't go to divinity school in the Church of God in Christ. You got a call when the Lord told you that you were needed in the ministry. Daddy got that call and within a couple of years was ordained and licensed.

My Parents: Lucy and Ben Harris

His first church was in a place called Ogden, near the Texas border. The whole family rode in Daddy's car all the way down there to meet the congregants and see what their church was like. Daddy took a look around and quickly decided that he would build his first church. You have to start somewhere.

And the congregants impressed him, all three or four of them! Daddy took seriously his Biblical instruction: "For where two or three are gathered in my name, there am I in the midst of them" (Matthew 18:20).

So, every weekend, on narrow two-lane U.S. Highway 67, we made the hundred-mile trip to Ogden to build the church and watch Daddy develop his pastoring skills in the home of Sister Irene, the mother of the church. And then it was another hundred miles back home. After several months, the church was constructed and named the Harris Temple Church of God in Christ, Ogden, Arkansas. Daddy later moved to larger churches closer to home.

Every two or three years, Daddy always seemed to find a way to purchase a new automobile. Cars were necessary to his work, but the man loved *nice* ones. Ultimately, he ended up, as did many Black ministers in those days, on the Cadillac track. I would say that, for the last twenty years of his life, he was dedicated to owning a late-model Cadillac. I suppose that as he became better known within the church structure, and ultimately was appointed a superintendent with his own jurisdiction, he had to project an image of being a successful preacher. Some folks do associate eminence with affluence. You have to look the part. And I suspect that at that late stage in his life, when he had raised five children and managed to save a good amount of money—for Frugality was his middle name—he figured, "Why not?" A Cadillac was the one and only luxury I ever knew him to afford himself.

One of the most important early memories of church for me was a convocation in 1950 at the Church of God in Christ in Arkadelphia, pastored at that time by Elder O. N. Dennis.

The church was located at the dead end of a street in the colored section of town, but to me at the time it appeared to be huge, compared to our little church in Manchester. It was at that church one Saturday evening that I received my first standing ovation, when I was six years old.

As the story goes, it was all Mother's plan. One day, she said to me, "Robert Lewis, I want you to memorize the names of all the books of the Bible."

I'm not sure I asked *why* just then, but the reason did reveal itself: Mother was planning to show me off at the convocation.

Now, learning all sixty-six titles in correct order might sound daunting, but I believed I could do it because Mother believed I could do it, and Mother was never wrong.

She had my performance staged perfectly. First, I was to recite the book titles of the Old Testament, pause for a few seconds to catch my breath and to switch gears, and then proceed with the book titles of the New Testament. The intent was to have maximum theatrical effect.

I practiced the names of the books of the Old Testament, starting with Genesis and ending with Malachi. Pronouncing the names of some of the books presented the greatest challenge. For example, titles like Obadiah, Habakkuk, Zephaniah and Haggai were tongue twisters. Reciting the names of the books of the shorter New Testament, commencing with Matthew and ending with Revelation, was a whole lot easier. It took several weeks of practice before I mastered the task, just in time for the convocation.

The morning of the day of the event, Mother cooked a big breakfast. "Eat good, Robert Lewis," she said. "Tonight is a big night."

When we arrived at church around six in the evening, I can remember seeing cars parked seemingly everywhere on the dead-end street. I had never seen so many cars and so many people at a church, which was exciting. Something bigger than I had imagined was about to happen, but I wasn't scared. I just kept reciting the titles over and over again in my head to assure myself that I had them in order.

At the beginning of the program, it was announced, without revealing exactly what was coming, that the small son of Elder Ben Harris and Sister Lucy Harris would be giving a special performance. Momentum was building, but I was cool. Maybe that had to do with the fact that I had seen my Daddy over and over again stand up and preach to people. There was nothing scary about his performances, so why should *I* be afraid? Fear, I know, isn't rational, but I just didn't have it.

Around 8:00 P.M., the minister in charge of the program proudly announced, "Tonight, we have a six-year-old boy, Robert Harris, who is going to recite the titles of all of the books of the Bible."

Immediately, there was applause. I was ready—as ready as I could be. With my best clothes on, I quickly walked to the front of the church, near the pulpit, where I could be seen, and said, "My name is Robert Harris, and these are the books of the Old Testament."

All eyes were glued on me. I could feel a growing love and support exuding from the congregation, and was energized by it.

After reciting the books of the Old Testament, I dramatically paused for a moment, as Mother had directed me to, and proceeded by saying, "And now the books of the New

Testament."

I then commenced with the book of Matthew and ended with Revelation, at which point a thunderous applause erupted. The congregation rose to its feet and clapped for a very long time. I came away from that experience firmly believing that learning had rewards.

In my earliest memories, I can hear my parents impressing upon me the importance of getting an education and "making something of yourself." Time and time again, and seemingly every day, I was reminded by them, "Boy, an education is something they can't take from you." Obviously, the "they" was a reference to White folks and the entrenched system of segregation that permeated every aspect of our lives. My parents clearly understood that for anyone living in a completely segregated Arkansas, education was most likely the only escape into a world with greater opportunity. Education was the key. For me, it began in a two-room schoolhouse called Williams Elementary.

5

They Can't Take My Education

None of us got where we are solely by pulling ourselves up by our bootstraps. We got here because somebody—a parent, a teacher, an Ivy League crony or a few nuns—bent down and helped us pick up our boots.

—Thurgood Marshall

Little if any written history exists on Williams Elementary School, located in Manchester. What we children were told was that the school was named after Shandy Williams, who was born a slave in Alabama in 1844. Shandy migrated to Manchester, where he fathered twenty children, the youngest being twins, Jacob and Joseph, who donated the land on which both the Church of God in Christ and the school were located, right next door to each other. The Williams twins, who were prominent figures in the area, were brothers to my grandmother, Mary Williams Harris. Even though our community is officially called Manchester, there's a little sign on the road leading into it today that says, "Williamstown."

My earliest memory of Williams Elementary School goes back to 1949, when I enrolled in the first grade. I was in the classroom for grades one through four; the other one being for grades five through eight. The structure was a two-room shack with a wood-burning stove in each room. We had well water and an outhouse. Small as the school was, it accommodated our community. And limited as our educational tools may have been (we studied from discarded books handed down to us from the better-funded schools for Whites), our teachers were determined that we would learn. They had their ways, but the one thing they had in common was a firm belief in encouragement.

Williams Elementary School

Each class had five or six kids, so each room had approximately twenty kids per teacher. When time came for a class to make one of its two daily presentations, the teacher would tell the kids to come to the front rows, while the other three grades would remain in their seats reading, doing assignments, or preparing for their own presentations. Thus, each class would be given one hour on the front row, with the morning half of the school day commencing at 8:00 A.M. and ending at noon. After lunch, this process would be repeated. So, there were only two hours per day that we were actually before the teacher. During those hours, several subjects were covered, my favorites being English and History. I loved to read and took great pleasure in memorizing the names of important historical people, places, things, and dates.

While the other classes were presenting, silence was strictly enforced. If we were to disrupt the room with noise, we knew that would require a whipping with a branch from one of the trees outside the school. Often, the "switch" would lie on top of the teacher's desk as a visual reminder of the consequences of disruption. Occasionally, someone—usually one of the boys—would test the teacher. But when the rest of us observed the consequences, we would decide it was just foolish to engage in that behavior because of the certainty of swift punishment. The teachers had the full permission of the law and all of the parents to discipline us physically, but that wasn't the end of it. If we misbehaved, they would tell our parents, and we would get a second punishment, another whipping. For the most part, this double punishment deterred disruptive behavior.

The two teachers, both Black, were Miss Evelyn College, a slightly chubby, nurturing woman, who taught grades one through four, and the petite Miss S. A. Braggs, who taught grades five through eight with Napoleonic zeal.

I was the teacher's pet of Miss College, who rewarded my efforts with an invitation to spend a weekend with her and her family in their home in Arkadelphia when I was around eight. That was the first time I spent a weekend away from my own home, and I thoroughly enjoyed it. The College family had indoor toilets and running water, cold and hot. Up till then, I had no idea how to use such facilities.

There would be more such visits to Miss College's home and those of others who gave me my first real taste of how life was lived outside the country. Those visits changed me, for I began to dream of one day moving away to a place where I wouldn't have to pick cotton. And I was further motivated in that direction by visits from relatives. It was always impressive to see my uncles and aunts come to our home in nice cars, well dressed and looking as if they didn't belong out in the cotton fields. It was hard to see my cousins leave at summer's end.

My Aunt Viola, a teacher, and Uncle Steve, a principal, who lived in Jonesboro, Arkansas, would visit for a bit with their two daughters, Joyce and Everne. Those privileged girls knew nothing of the hard work we had to do out in the country. I wasn't jealous—or maybe I was a little bit—but whenever they came, I actually found it motivating and thought more and more of what it would be like to move away. Jonesboro was not a large city, but it was not the country. I dreamed of going to Arkansas A&M, at the time a major Black college, located in Pine Bluff, and becoming an educator like Aunt Viola and Uncle Steve.

Another relative who would come down to visit was Uncle Robert, the uncle I was named after, Daddy's oldest brother. Uncle Robert would drive down from the Chicago area, always looking handsome and prosperous. He was an electrician who had done quite well because he was a good businessman. I dreamed of being like him one day.

On Mother's side, there were relatives who had gone off to other places and appeared to be prosperous. One was Aunt

Dora, Mother's older sister. When I was eleven or twelve, my parents put me on a train to visit her. Aunt Dora lived in a comfortable home in Little Rock. I remember she had a fig tree in the backyard, and since I had never seen one of those before, I took some time looking at it before I got used to the idea that I could eat the figs. I enjoyed them immensely. To my wide country eyes, Aunt Dora's home was beautiful.

Another relative on Mother's side who showed me what life could be like beyond the country was Uncle Ridley Luster, whose name was actually Charlie. He was essentially illiterate, but he did very well as a businessman selling timber. Uncle Ridley would contract his services to cut logs and haul them to a mill in his big truck. He married a schoolteacher named Aunt Dessie. It was always good to visit their immaculate home in Arkadelphia. We could go there often because they were nearby.

So, I had plenty of motivation to dream that one day I could have the kind of luxuries that I saw in their homes— the indoor toilets and the bathtubs with running water. All of those relatives really motivated me to study hard, which I did. Indeed, I loved school. My first teacher had fundamentally changed my life.

After fourth grade, it was time to move on to a different teacher, but one who would be equally influential in my development. Although Miss College had been firm, everybody knew that Miss Braggs did not take any stuff. Some of us thought she was just a little crazy. Over the years, she had earned a well-deserved reputation as subscribing to the biblical philosophy of "Spare the rod, spoil the child." She didn't hesitate for a minute to administer harsh discipline for infractions in her classroom.

On more than one occasion, she called the boys who disrespected decorum "darkies," which was somewhat disconcerting because she herself was dark-skinned. Miss Braggs proceeded to discipline those boys with her infamous switch, which was notably larger than Miss College's—almost twice the diameter and length. Not only did Miss Braggs use the switch to maintain "law and order," but she also used it as a source of "motivation" for those kids who didn't do their homework or whom she thought were lazy. She fervently believed that everybody in her classroom could learn.

I had no fear of transitioning to fifth grade, for two reasons. First, I was too afraid to disrupt the class because of that switch; and second, I believed that I was smart and thus would always be ready to excel in Miss Braggs's classroom. Unfortunately, some of my classmates were not as well prepared, so I had to witness the administration of "motivation" to them more than once.

Looking back, I realize that Miss Braggs's disciplinary measures were rather harsh, but the results were that no child graduated from Williams Elementary School who did not know how to read, write, and do simple math. Moreover, none of the parents ever complained about the tactics, and were very supportive, so the kids did not have the option of going home to complain about a teacher's disciplinary practices.

Long after I graduated from Williams Elementary School, Miss Braggs's tenacious belief in the innate ability of all students to learn stayed with me. She was fundamentally persuaded that if we applied ourselves and studied hard, there would be no significant barriers to our ability to compete with others. She had high expectations of all her students, even though their individual capacities varied. Most of all, she inspired us to learn and achieve. At almost every juncture of my educational journey, the one common thread has always been the level of confidence that Miss Braggs instilled in me.

She would often admonish us that our only limits were those we imposed on ourselves. Whether or not we graduated from high school, she cared less about us being country kids in rural Manchester than about our developing our minds. "Be the best you can be" was often her motto, and it was that belief in my own ability to learn that struck a chord with me, reinforcing what Mother was so sure of and Daddy had preached.

Graduating from Williams Elementary was a moment of joy for me, but yet a time of sadness, too. Our ceremony— to the extent that it could be called such—was very small and without fanfare. I had been encouraged, recognized, and protected in our little Manchester community and its colored school, but now I had to move on to Arkadelphia, to our school district's only secondary school for colored students, Peake High School, where hundreds of us were bussed in from around the district.

Built in 1929, Peake High was named after J. Edward Peake, the White landowner who had donated two acres for the only high school for Blacks in Clark County. Located at 1600 Caddo Street, the school was a forty-five-minute ride from Manchester. I would catch the school bus each day, after walking a quarter of a mile from home up the often muddy dirt road to the main road, also dirt, where I would be picked up.

At age thirteen, in September 1957, I enrolled in ninth grade, along with my classmates from Williams Elementary

School. At the same time, following the 1954 U.S. Supreme Court decision in *Brown v. Board of Education*, the first attempt to desegregate a secondary public school in the state of Arkansas was being made at Central High School in Little Rock, sixty miles away.

Nine colored students, who became known as the Little Rock Nine, enrolled at Central High, but a mob of angry White people rioted to prevent integration. The Arkansas National Guard was called in by the governor, who was determined to keep Central High segregated. Ultimately, President Eisenhower, after a couple of weeks of nonintervention, federalized the Arkansas National Guard, instructing it to guarantee the safe attendance of the Little Rock Nine at Central High.

As the world focused on the chaos in Little Rock, I enrolled in my ninth-grade courses peacefully, largely unaware of what was happening in the capital. Seldom was there any talk about it, as if we were on some distant planet, miles from Central High and the courageous Little Rock Nine. Those students were paving the way for unraveling the threads of segregation that consumed the state and many others across the nation. Our segregated school system in Arkadelphia remained intact and unchallenged. In fact, Arkadelphia's public schools were thoroughly segregated until the 1969–1970 school year, at which time all public schools in the state were integrated.

In any case, when I entered high school, the all-colored Peake, I wasn't thinking about integration or colored versus White. My first bus rides across the Ouachita River represented a major social, not racial, passage. Students who lived in Arkadelphia referred to us as "the students from across the river." Although silly, this was their feeble attempt to give themselves higher status as city dwellers, while labeling us as being country—which, of course, we were. Despite that attempt to demean us, I wasn't impacted at all. Actually, it motivated me to be even more competitive, just to show them that although I was from "across the river," I could still outwit them.

My ninth-grade classes at Peake High were huge, compared to those I had been in at Williams Elementary. There were fifty or more students in my class (ten times what I had been accustomed to), who were divided into two evenly distributed sections. At first, I felt a little uncertain about how I would do competitively, because I was up against more students. But I had a secret weapon, having come from the tenacious Miss Braggs, who had convinced me that there was no mountain I couldn't climb in the educational arena. All I needed to do was study like hell. And I did just that.

Peake High had a remarkable principal, who was respected throughout the Black community. Mr. Nathaniel Bacon Cooke, a tall, lanky, imposing figure, could possibly have passed as a White man, thanks to his extremely light complexion and stern demeanor, but there was nothing threatening about him. He was, in fact, a caring educator, who believed firmly in strict discipline, and he closely nurtured those who wanted to graduate and go on to college. I was in that group.

Several other teachers stand out in my memory. First, Mr. Jerome Muldrew, whose wife taught home economics at Peake, was the physical education instructor. He was very supportive of me. Years later, our paths crossed frequently, after I graduated from college and was active in my fraternity,

Kappa Alpha Psi, which I later learned was also his fraternity. We remembered each other, so as I ran for national offices in the fraternity, I could always count on him to deliver the Arkansas vote for me.

My favorite science teacher, Mr. C. B. Blevins, was regarded by the students as the most difficult instructor at Peake High. He taught general science, biology, chemistry, and physics. Students tried to avoid his classes because of his strict grading. Mr. Blevins was a very thin man, who stood at almost six feet. He was noted for his precise lectures, usually from notes, and for his propensity to require lots of memorizing—which, of course, I was good at. Although, due to the cotton-picking season, I had to miss a number of days at the beginning of the school year, I was able to get his lecture notes from another student and catch up with the class. By the end of the first half of the school year, around December, I was doing quite well in his course. And by the end of the school year, despite missing more days to chop cotton, I ended up near the top of the class, which made me one of his favorites, earning me special status among other students, especially those who were too afraid to take his classes.

Another teacher who left a lasting impression on me was my woodshop instructor, Mr. M. D. Caesar. He was an older man, who believed in hand-paddling if you didn't do your homework correctly. He introduced his classes, which were all for boys, to the 4-H Clubs of America, which focused on agricultural issues, especially the planting and managing of trees, as well as other matters of importance to the rural way of life. Among other things, Mr. Caesar had a penchant for singing and tried to teach his students how to carry a tune.

Unfortunately, I was hopeless at that, so I failed miserably.

One of Mr. Caesar's favorite songs was "Summertime" from *Porgy and Bess* by George Gershwin, which Mr. Caesar tried to teach us, but I could never replicate the melody. The lyrics didn't resonate with me, either. I guess I couldn't relate to the life the song depicted:

Summertime, and the livin' is easy.

Not exactly, if you're picking cotton and have to miss school.

Oh, your daddy's rich and your ma is good-lookin'.

My mother was beautiful alright, and not just to me, but my Daddy sure wasn't rich—although we weren't poor, either. Clearly, we had less than some others, like an outhouse compared to my classmates' indoor bathrooms in their homes in town, but Daddy worked hard. As I pointed out earlier, he also really liked cars. Long before he allowed himself his first Cadillac, he managed to buy and maintain two of them—one that he drove to work, and the other that he used to travel to church on Sundays. That gave us *some* status!

The car that stands out most in my mind was his 1957 green Plymouth, which was boosted up in the rear with extra springs that Daddy had inserted. The car had two "wings" at the rear fenders, which made it look as if it were about to fly off into the air. Today, people would probably take one look at that car and think it belonged to a gangster. But there was a reason for it being raised up in the rear. It had to accommodate the weight of many passengers, for we were a big family, and there were always people jammed into the back seat. I don't know how Daddy figured this out perfectly, but he was very proud of his customized Plymouth.

My brother Leonard, on the other hand, wasn't as enthusiastic as Daddy was about the car. While he liked its looks, the Plymouth was more an instrument of excitement to him because of its speed. Leonard had gotten his driver's license at age fourteen; and by sixteen, he was considered a seasoned driver with a good driving record—although he had an informal reputation for speeding. Leonard denied the rumors, assuring my parents otherwise.

In addition to the 1957 Plymouth, Daddy had an old black 1951 Chevrolet that was his work car. Because Mother never learned to drive, Leonard was mostly responsible for driving her wherever she wanted to go. The fringe benefit was that Leonard would get to drive the new car because Daddy used the old one for going to work. Running errands for Mother often provided the chance to be alone in the new car, especially if Mother wanted something from the store, but didn't want to go along for the ride.

Almost instinctively, Daddy didn't trust Leonard with his car and sought clever means to track his driving. But Leonard was equally determined to match Daddy's cleverness in tracking his driving habits. Well aware of the rumors about Leonard's speeding, Daddy would check the car's odometer almost on a daily basis to be sure of the mileage, which would give him an estimate of any excessive usage to indicate that Leonard had been taking advantage of his driving privileges. Then he would tell Mother that Leonard had been "running around," and not just going to the store.

"Leonard," Mother would say, "have you been driving this car more than just to the store?"

"No," Leonard would say, wondering who was telling on him.

Daddy had a superb memory, so he never had to write anything down on paper, which meant that he always remembered the exact mileage of the car as he had left it. At first, Leonard was confounded by Daddy's knowledge, but he sort of ignored it, thinking that it must be divine knowledge on Daddy's part—perhaps part of his preaching powers. But as time went on, and as Daddy asked more and more questions, Leonard found it increasingly difficult to come up with cogent explanations.

Finally, Leonard said to me, "Robert, I've figured out why Daddy always knows how far I've driven his car."

"You have?"

"Yep."

"Why?"

"Have you noticed that every time he leaves, he always looks in the car on the driver's side..., and when he comes back, he does the same thing?"

"No, not really."

"Well, when he sticks his head in the car, he's really looking at the odometer, checking the mileage. And when he comes back, he does it again."

Having figured out Daddy's source of wisdom, Leonard shared with me his strategy to outfox our father.

"I know how to unscrew the odometer," he said. "So I can disconnect it when the number of miles Daddy anticipates the car should have been driven is reached. And then I can reconnect it right before I get home after one of my escapades."

Not long after that, Daddy quit questioning Leonard about where he had been, fairly comfortable that Leonard was not doing any unauthorized driving. In fact, Leonard was going anywhere and everywhere he pleased, now that he had figured out how not to get caught.

All good things must come to an end, and for Leonard that happened on a Saturday afternoon in late October 1957. When he asked Daddy if he and I could use the Plymouth to go over to Uncle Billy's, who lived a few miles away and had a number of kids our age, he promised that he would go no further than Delark, a small rural town only a few miles from Uncle Billy's home.

We did go to Uncle Billy's, at which point Leonard disconnected the odometer.

"I'll put it back," he said to me, "when we return here, just before going home. That way, Daddy will think we came over here and didn't go too far away. He won't mind if we go ten or fifteen miles more."

"What about the gas?" I asked. "Won't he see that it's too low?"

"We'll put some in," he said.

After spending a little time at Uncle Billy's house, we decided that it would be fun to go down to Sparkman in Dallas County, which was ten miles away. Confident that he had mastered the skill of hiding the car's mileage, Leonard drove me and five of our teenage cousins to Sparkman, with three of us in the front and four in the back. We cruised around the colored high school in Sparkman, where my cousins attended, and everything was good.

After calculating the number of miles the car should have on it after we returned home, Leonard pulled into a gas station in Sparkman, pumped in two gallons of fuel, and reconnected the odometer for the return trip. But as we were leaving town, laughing and having a good time, he unintentionally ran a stop sign just as we were passing the city limits. We thought nothing of it, but within seconds, we heard a siren, looked back, and saw flashing red lights. It was the Dallas County Sheriff's Department.

Knowing that he was not supposed to be down in the Sparkman area, Leonard figured that if he got a ticket there, Daddy would realize what was happening.

"Y'all hold on!" he said. "I can outrun the police."

At that point, he floored the gas pedal, and the wings of that Plymouth seemed to flap as if the car were about to take off. When I looked through the back windshield, I could see the white face of the police officer. I think all the law enforcement officers in Arkansas were White at that time.

This is it! I thought.

All my life, I had been taught to fear the wrath of White people. Manchester was essentially an all-Black community, where we felt safe. We had dealings with White folks, working for them and buying from them as needs be, but we were taught to always be on guard. My brothers and I learned that all of us were "boys" to White folks, and we would never grow up to be "men" in their eyes. Segregation was a way of life. We didn't like it, but we were taught to fear the consequences. We were particularly taught to fear the police. I was told that if you disobeyed them, bad things would happen. The best you could do was to follow orders and move on.

Leonard knew all that, but in that moment of extreme fear and panic, he pressed the accelerator and apparently hit the "passing gear," because the car suddenly made a roaring noise, and the speedometer, as I glanced at it, hit 90!

Sitting in the middle of the front seat, I was terrified, fearful that we would crash into something or turn over, so I got down on the floor of the car, hoping to shield myself in anticipation of a disaster. And I knew what a disaster looked like, because one of our cousins had been in a car wreck caused by speeding on the very same road we were on, and now he was paralyzed from the waist down.

But nothing was stopping Leonard. That Plymouth continued to accelerate until someone in the back seat shouted, "Shorty, we're outrunning them!"

That gave Leonard incentive to drive even faster.

I raised my head up momentarily to peek at the speedometer, which was now at 110!! I just knew my life was over. But when I heard the sound of the car transitioning from the pavement to a dusty dirt road, and Leonard finally began to decelerate, I calmed down.

God has spared my life! I said to myself.

Visibly shaken, I quickly got off the floor and back into my seat next to Leonard. The danger was over, and he was now a hero for having outrun the police.

As we all cheered, Leonard said with a smile, "I showed *them.*"

He was defiant and proud of his feat. But he got us all to agree that we wouldn't tell anyone about this incident.

When Leonard and I got home, we noticed that the other

car wasn't there, which meant that Daddy wasn't home. We both gave off a big sigh of relief and set about washing the Plymouth, which was colored brown by the dust.

As we finished washing the car, Daddy drove up, seeming quite pleased that Leonard had taken the initiative to wash the car after being allowed to use it. I watched nervously as Daddy walked up to the car, opened the front driver-side door, and sat there for a few seconds, obviously calculating the mileage. Apparently it computed, because he didn't have a frown on his face. Everything appeared to be going just right. Leonard had outsmarted a White Southern cop and Daddy, too. I was impressed.

But about an hour later, I noticed some dust coming from the road leading to our house. The sight of dust indicated that a car was coming, but that wasn't unusual. We did have visitors from time to time.

Leonard was in the house, but Daddy was sitting on the front porch, reading his Bible, as was his custom. As the dust came closer, I could see that the car had red lights on top, which made my heart sink to my feet.

As the Dallas County sheriff's car drove into the yard, Daddy raised his head, looking surprised, obviously wondering, *Why is he here?*

The sheriff slowly opened his car door, put on his hat, and walked up to the Plymouth. After looking at it briefly, he proceeded to the porch, where Daddy was now standing with a puzzled look on this face.

"Is this your car?" the sheriff asked.

"Yes, sir," Daddy replied.

"Was your son driving this car earlier this afternoon?"

"Yes, sir."

"I'm here to arrest him for speeding."

Immediately, Daddy hollered into the house, "Leonard, boy, get out here right now!"

When Leonard came out, the sheriff said, "Boy, you're coming with me!"

With all of us, including Mother, watching, frozen in helplessness, the sheriff drove away with Leonard in the back seat, and Daddy following behind in the Plymouth.

While I don't know the details of what happened at the sheriff's office in Sparkman, I do know that, about three hours later, Daddy and Leonard arrived back at the house, where Mother was anxiously waiting on the lighted porch.

Leonard never talked about it, at least not to me. But one thing's for certain—it never happened again.

It wasn't until many years later that we realized that the Dallas County sheriff didn't even have jurisdiction to make an arrest in Clark County. But had Daddy realized that at the time, what could he have done differently? You didn't talk back to a White man, especially one with a badge and a gun. And that's still good advice.

That terrifying experience served to give me another reason to work really hard at my studies. Education, as I had been taught and fervently believed, was my path to freedom—freedom from the tentacles of segregation, a system that demanded that I live in paralyzing fear of White men. I wanted out; my sister and brothers also wanted out; and my parents, though they would miss us, wanted us out, too.

6

View from the Back of the Bus

*I was leaving the South
to fling myself into the unknown...
I was taking a part of the South
to transplant in alien soil,
to see if it could grow differently,
if it could drink of new and cool rains,
bend in strange winds,
respond to the warmth of other suns
and, perhaps, to bloom.*

—Richard Wright

In the late 1950s, this country was changing ever so slowly in its racial policies—too slowly for a lot of Black folks. Prejudice and a lack of opportunity in the South had already led to decades of the Great Migration north and west. In my extended family, on Daddy's side, we were already well scattered, with most settling in California.

The first person in Daddy's immediate family to head west was Uncle Leonard. He had served in the army during World War II, and while headed to the Pacific battlefields, had gotten his first glimpse of the San Francisco Bay Area when he was stationed at the Oakland Army Base, a major transit point. He must have really liked what he saw, because he relocated after the war to the Bay Area, specifically to Pittsburg, about thirty miles northeast of Oakland.

Almost every summer, Uncle Leonard—or Lemard, as we called him—would make the long drive back home to Manchester with his wife, Aunt Sybil. They didn't have any children, but they were instrumental in the lives of their nieces and nephews.

My sister Jean's last summer in Manchester followed her first year in college. She had been one of several colored students who attended Henderson State Teachers' College in 1958, after it had quietly been integrated the previous year. The enrollment of colored students had been completed without news cameras or any trouble. Despite that accomplishment, when Aunt Ernestine, one of Daddy's older sisters, suggested that Jean should return to Oakland, California, with her, Jean didn't hesitate. She intended to further her education in California, which my parents liked, but she didn't plan on coming back.

Shortly after Jean arrived in Oakland, Uncle Lemard and Aunt Sybil invited her to come live with them in Pittsburg. Oakland was a considerably bigger city, with an exciting night life and a growing colored community of migrants from the South, but Uncle Lemard somehow persuaded Jean that she would be better off in Pittsburg. Nevertheless, four months later, Uncle Lemard paid for her to live in San Francisco for eight months to attend Heald Business College. After that, Jean returned to Oakland to live with Aunt Gladys and her husband, Uncle Charles. She then convinced my brother Leonard that he needed to take her place in Uncle Lemard's home in Pittsburg. The year was 1959, and Leonard had only one year left at Peake High, but he chose to head west anyway, and completed school at Pittsburg High.

Meanwhile, Jean turned her attention to a man she had to literally look up to—Artis Blacksher, who stood 6'-4" and weighed not an ounce less than 250 pounds. Jean married him in June 1960, but that didn't end her campaign to get all of her brothers out of Arkansas. Three months after saying, "I do," she told Mother that she wanted me to come live with her and Artis in Oakland.

I learned of Jean's invitation on a hot, humid summer afternoon as I arrived home from work. I had been tossing bales of hay into a slowly moving truck all day. I remember Mother standing on the front porch as I got out from behind the wheel of Daddy's car and headed to the house. She appeared to be waiting for me, for no reason that I could discern from the expression on her face, but I sensed that she had something to tell me.

"Your sister wants…," she began, and then paused. "You don't wanna go to California, do you?"

She really wasn't expecting me to answer, because she already knew what I would say. I *had* to go, we *all* had to go, to fulfill the dreams that she and Daddy had planted in us. But it hurt her. She didn't break down in hysterics, although I could feel her sorrow. Or maybe it was just resignation, a painful acceptance. There was no sense in fighting the inevitable.

Daddy, on the other hand, was stoic. He was not going to engage emotionally in trying to keep me home. He knew what was coming. I would go.

Three years later, child number four, Harold, would follow

me, enlisting in the army in Oakland, and ultimately settling in Detroit.

Finally, the baby, Charlie, reached Oakland. That was Jean's most delicate extraction, but I had a hand in it, too.

It was 1967. My parents and Charlie visited Oakland that summer, and we all had a wonderful time. When the trip was over, Jean persuaded Mother and Daddy to let Charlie stay for a couple of extra weeks. By the time their bus reached Arkansas, Jean and I had convinced Charlie to stay in California to complete his last year of high school.

When Daddy heard the news, he was neutral, but Mother was none too pleased. She wanted her baby, her last child, back in the nest. It wasn't to be, although Charlie would give my parents something to brag about. After excelling at Castlemont High School in Oakland, he won a full scholarship to Stanford University, on his way to becoming a civil engineer.

So, everything worked out well for me and my sister and brothers—the migration, that is. But I had no way of knowing that when I stepped on a Continental Trailways bus in the summer of 1960 to begin my westward journey. I left just one day after being told that Jean had invited me, so I could enroll on time at a high school in Oakland. Mother and Daddy drove me to Arkadelphia and bought me a one-way ticket. There was no time to get used to the idea that I was leaving, and no time for second-guessing. It was just happening.

Before boarding, I took one last look at my mother, who had tears in her eyes. Much like Jean, I was strong-willed, but there was also the fear of the unknown pulsating in my heart. Here I was, a sixteen-year-old, heading to an unknown place, two thousand miles away. Everything I owned was tightly packed in a small suitcase made of cardboard, so flimsy that I could have sliced it with a dull knife. No trinkets, no photos—just a few pairs of pants, several shirts, underwear, and socks. My only shoes were on my feet.

When I got on the bus in Arkadelphia, I walked straight to the back, just as I knew I had to. I would have been put off and maybe arrested had I tried to sit in front. That was okay with me. I had a view, and as the bus passed through cities unknown to me, my excitement grew.

When we passed the border into New Mexico from Texas, our first stop was Tucumcari, where the driver announced that passengers could sit anywhere they wanted. That was my first time out of the South, my first taste of freedom. I didn't move. I guess that I was a little reticent, having never sat in the front of a bus, but I also was quite comfortable where I was. I liked my view from the back of the bus.

7

Bright Lights Can Deceive

I have a rendezvous with life.

—Countee Cullen

When I reached California, the first place that I remember seeing was hazy Los Angeles—although it didn't make much of an impression, I think, because I was so close to my future home, so focused on imagining what my new world in the Bay Area would look like, that L.A. didn't matter. The final leg of the seemingly endless road trip, some 330 miles to the north, brought me into downtown Oakland just after dark to the unremarkable bus station at Twentieth Street and San Pablo Avenue, which is still there today.

My first impression of Oakland was brightness. In a metaphorical sense, yes, I was moving from segregation to integration, from the imprisoned dark to the hopeful light. But my thoughts were less philosophical and more emotional—like the moment that electric lights went on for the first time in Manchester. Literally. Oakland had lights at night. Wow! That was new for me. Plus the city was larger than any place I had ever seen. (I was half-asleep when I passed through

Los Angeles in the morning.) Little Rock, the capital of Arkansas, was the biggest city I had previously visited, but it wasn't very developed at that time, particularly in the colored neighborhoods, which were certainly not as bright as Oakland after dark.

Excited as I was when I thought about seeing my sister again, I wasn't the least bit let down by not finding Jean and Artis at the station, waiting for me, because they had told me they would be working late that day. My welcoming party consisted of my cousin, Roosevelt Harris, who courteously met me and kindly drove me to my sister's home in his smashing black 1956 Ford Fairlane, which was so polished that it looked brand new. Although Daddy had owned some nice cars, this was the most beautiful car I had ever seen.

Jean and Artis

Jean and Artis lived in a one-bedroom apartment at 1064 Fifty-third Street at San Pablo Avenue in north Oakland. I recall it being smaller than the home I had left behind in Arkansas, but not by much. In the living room, though, there was a new full-size convertible couch that became my bed. It was the first bed of my own and surely the largest.

The day after my arrival, Artis dropped me off to enroll at Oakland Technical High School on Broadway. The dazzling white-stone, two-story building with imposing Greek columns had been built in 1914, and occupied an entire block. It was the largest school building I had ever seen. As I headed to the entrance, I was swept forward in a crowd of roughly two thousand students, four times as many as I had encountered at my old school. They were overwhelmingly different, too, since almost all of them were White, and only ten percent were Black. But, honestly, when I think back to how I felt on that first day, I don't recall being at all intimidated.

This experience was something new, so there was fear of the unknown racing through my nervous system, but I felt no self-doubt. I wasn't threatened by this overwhelmingly White world I was entering, even though I had never before had any interaction with White kids. Not in school, not at work, not at church, and not in the fields of play. My world was changing, but I was still the same little boy who memorized the names of the books of the Bible and stood up before a large congregation to recite them. Given an opportunity, I knew I could perform. I was excited.

As I walked into the school, I was of one mind. Enrollment. I had come to California with a singular mission: to attend college. My sister had explained to me that I would need to take college preparatory classes in order to get there.

Although I had no idea where I was headed, I luckily found the Office of the Registrar without any problems. No one had to guide me. The counselor I approached was the first White school official I ever interacted with—or even had the opportunity to speak with. Her name was Mrs. Miriam Hillegas, a middle-aged White woman with graying hair.

As we exchanged courteous greetings, her tone wasn't officious or imposing, but kind. Since enrollment was based on where you lived, I explained that I was now living in the neighborhood. She gave me a card to fill out, on which I was to choose my classes. As proof of my prior high school record, I handed her a transcript of my courses and grades from Peake High. I had an A-minus average, and let Mrs. Hillegas know that I had been the number two student in my class. Number one was my cousin, Orlando Macon, who seemed to always be able to beat me, no matter what. Still, I wasn't far behind him.

I was smiling—boasting, I guess, in an approval-seeking way. After I handed Mrs. Hillegas my enrollment card, and she read the college prep courses that I had checked, she looked up at me perplexed, as if I had shot her with a stun gun. Her confusion was all over her face. I was confused, too, and clearly she could see that, so she gently explained to me that even though I had done well in high school in Arkansas, there was no way I would be able to "keep up" with students in college prep courses in California, and I had chosen the most challenging classes at that.

Then she took out a blank enrollment card and wrote down a number of courses that she thought I should take, none of which were college prep—classes like woodshop and art.

Clearly, from her "now, now, child" tone of voice, I suspected that she thought she was doing me a favor. She certainly wasn't trying to hurt my feelings. But there was to be no backtalk. She was quite firm, and I couldn't think of anything I could say to change her mind.

Mrs. Hillegas didn't even pretend to hide her belief that I couldn't compete in the most academically challenging courses. That was a big letdown for me—my first experience of low expectations, and it was an eye-opener. Although I was stunned, I figured I would ultimately win this battle because I knew my sister. At that moment, though, I had no choice other than to capitulate—without displaying any hostile emotion. I had to accept the counselor's signed enrollment card, angrily attend the classes she had chosen for me, and later tell Jean all about it.

As I've implied, my sister takes no prisoners. She is a determined woman who speaks her mind. When I told her and Artis what had happened, Jean used very choice words, not complimentary at all, about *that* counselor, and quickly devised a plan, using her not-so-secret weapon: her husband.

"Make sure he gets enrolled in college-prep courses *tomorrow*," she told him.

I got the feeling that my brother-in-law was excited about that assignment. Artis, who had graduated from Berkeley High School, was accustomed to dealing with White folks, and had no fear of them—or anyone else, for that matter. Nature didn't make him that way. He was a truck driver, every bit as fearsome physically as Jean was verbally.

The next day, Artis drove me back to the school, but this time he didn't drop me off. When we both walked into the building, which was more like marching to battle, we headed straight for the counselor's office.

Mrs. Hillegas recognized me right away—this 5'-8" tall misguided colored boy she thought she had set straight the day before. She was stunned, however, to see the towering Black man next to me.

Artis didn't wait to be introduced. He immediately and firmly instructed Mrs. Hillegas to enroll me in college-prep courses, making it clear from his looks and gestures that this was not to be a debate. In fact, there wouldn't be a compromise, either. The counselor had only one choice: enroll me in those courses, or else. He never said that, but Mrs. Hillegas got the message rather quickly. Not at all happy, she mumbled something as she handed me a new enrollment form. I filled it out and put it right back in front of her to sign—which she did, and promptly handed it back to me.

No "Good luck," was extended. No "Come and see me anytime, if you have questions." No "Goodbye." But I didn't care. Her signature was what I needed, so I wasn't at all hurt by her dismissive, sour expression, which said, "You're on your own, kid!"

Artis and I were smiling. The show was over.

This was the first time in my life that I had seen a Black person stand up to a White person—and in this case, without even a real fight, which I have to admit I half-expected. Having grown up in the snake-infested cotton fields of backwoods Arkansas, where I had only seen White people showing their dominance over Black people, this showdown was way more than fascinating. It was transformative. To say the least, Artis impressed me. This—my first battle with low expectations—

had ended in victory. Now anything was possible. The showdown reinforced something I already knew: I could fight and I could win.

For sixteen years, I had been led to believe by my parents that I was very smart, that I could achieve anything I wanted if I worked hard enough. The teachers in my segregated schools had also convinced me that I was smart, that my only limits would be self-imposed. That was the benefit of being educated in segregated schools. My sense of self-worth was molded by people who believed that I was every bit as capable as any competitor I was ever likely to face. It was a bit late in life to have that confidence shaken by one racially imprudent school counselor.

I was on track now, the right track. To be sure, it was interesting to attend classes in which almost all the students were White. Of the five hundred in my class, a small percentage took college-prep classes, and only a handful of those were Black, perhaps one or two percent. But, truthfully, from the very first day in that school, I never felt uncomfortable.

All the students had the same books. If the material we were studying was in those books, I would be able to read it, comprehend it, and thus be able to compete. Furthermore, none of the teachers in those college-prep courses had any negative attitudes toward me. They didn't know where I had come from or how I had come to be registered in their courses. I suspect that Mrs. Hillegas never told anyone about the controversy over my enrollment. Why would she? It would only make her look bad in the eyes of the more open-minded faculty. Therefore, my teachers presumed that since I was enrolled in their classes, I must be able to keep up.

Two teachers stand out as being particularly supportive and encouraging. The silver-haired Miss Helen Keller taught me English Literature, and clearly the concept of unequal racial expectations never entered her mind. She would mention my papers to the class as models of what she would like to see from everyone.

Mr. Vartanian, my World History teacher, was a gentleman from Turkey. He was a real character, with a thick mustache, dark olive skin, and jet-black hair, and was very energetic and animated as he addressed the class. His enthusiasm made World History exciting for all of us. He had great confidence in my abilities and would often call on me to recite historical facts or to recount historical events. I loved it. No one knows everything, but I did have a great memory, which I had known since I was six. Over and over, Mr. Vartanian gave me a chance to display that talent—not for its own sake, but to further a particular discussion. It wasn't about showing off; it was about connecting events by means of historical facts. My experience in Mr. Vartanian's class was so positive that in college I seriously considered majoring in history.

I don't recall if there were any other Black students in Mr. Vartanian's class, but there was one in Miss Keller's class. In fact, Pat Grogan was one of the most gorgeous girls I had ever seen, and I had a crush on her. Of course, I knew there was no way in the world that I had a chance of dating her, a poor little hick like me—from Arkansas in country clothes. But we were friends, and we studied together sometimes. That's about as close to having a girlfriend as I ever got at Oakland Tech. She probably knew that I was sweet on her, but she saw me as a friend, and we stayed that way for years.

Despite my being one of only a few Blacks in college prep, there were opportunities for me to make friendships with other Black students at the school. And indeed I did, even though I entered in the twelfth grade, long after firm friendships and cliques are usually formed. A few of my buddies at Oakland Tech became long-lasting friends.

At Oakland Tech, 12th grade

Robin and Lionel B. Wilson, who were identical twins, and one year behind me in school, were so light-skinned that I initially thought they were White. It took me at least two weeks to realize they were Black. Their father, Lionel J. Wilson, was a lawyer at that time, who went on to become a Municipal Court judge, then a Superior Court judge, and finally the first Black mayor of Oakland. Lionel B. and Robin also became lawyers later in life.

Malcolm and Mike Hunter also became longtime friends. Mike, who was the older of the two, was in a few college-prep courses with me. Like the Wilson brothers, the Hunter brothers ultimately became lawyers. By coincidence, Malcolm was briefly married to my cousin Charlene, my Aunt Gladys's daughter.

I was also a friend of Eddie Titus and Jim Henderson, both outstanding players on Oakland Tech's football team. How a college-prep country boy became friends with those two popular athletes is beyond me, but I came to know them quite well. Eddie won a scholarship to play football in college, and Jim went on with me to Merritt College.

The White students at Oakland Tech were not especially different from the Black students. I had casual friendships with a few of them, and don't recall any incidents of racism. The truth is that I felt comfortable with all the students I met, Black and White. I can't really explain why. For sure, I was different—dressed differently and spoke differently. I was a colored Arkansas country boy, and anyone could hear it. My jargon and points of reference were decidedly Southern. But the other students and I essentially spoke the same language because we had read the same books. We could communicate.

I did find college-prep to be more competitive than what I had previously experienced, but I performed well by spending more time than before on homework. It was a familiar challenge: having to play catch-up for so many years thanks to the time missed from school while picking cotton.

After I had been in the school for six months, I had another encounter with Mrs. Hillegas—and, in a way, she got her revenge. However sweet that may have been for her, in hindsight I'm not certain it was a bad thing for me.

Of course, Mrs. Hillegas was my counselor for the whole time I was at Oakland Tech. I had no choice other than to maintain a courteous but uncomfortable relationship with her.

When I consulted her about going to college, she had all the information and contacts, but chose to limit what to share with me, making certain not to expose me to any choices beyond community colleges. At the time, that included Oakland Junior College, which later became Oakland City College, and today is known as Merritt College. She never shared any information about more academically challenging universities, public or private, or even about the state colleges in the Bay Area.

At that time, I couldn't afford tuition on my own, my parents didn't have any extra funds, and my sister certainly didn't have any money to send me off to a big university. Therefore, going to community college or junior college seemed like a good option. That would cost perhaps twenty dollars a semester at most. And after two years, I could transfer to a four-year college—which I hoped would be San Francisco State College, now San Francisco State University.

8

My New Family

You don't choose your family. They are
God's gift to you, as you are to them.

—Desmond Tutu

I don't recall suffering any seriously rough patches of longing for home during my transition from Manchester to Oakland. Ambitious as I was, I fully embraced change, although that isn't to say I didn't have emotional needs. For sure, at times I sorely missed Mother's protective hugs, but, in truth, I had changed houses, not families. In my first two years in Oakland, relatives I already knew and some I would meet made the critical difference in my adjustment.

Jean happily became my substitute mother, and Artis my substitute father, and I was pleased to give them all the respect they deserved. They provided good counsel on what to do, what not to do, where to go, when to go there, and what time to be home.

We lived in the one-bedroom apartment with the pullout couch for a year. I helped to clean, but there wasn't much to scrub, since the place was so small. At first, washing dishes was my chore, something I could do with an appreciative smile, but more chores were to come.

Jean worked full-time in Berkeley in the dietary department at Alta Bates Hospital. (She would spend her entire career of nearly forty years there.) Soon after I arrived in 1960, she began taking in ironing for extra income. When it came to handling money, Artis followed her lead. It was Jean, Daddy's daughter, who passionately believed that a dollar saved is a dollar earned. She insisted on adhering to a budget, and was determined not to spend a penny on foolishness like fancy clothes and such. She even styled her own hair.

Jean had a plan to move up in the world. After I lived with her and Artis for a year, we moved to a two-bedroom apartment at 1611 Ward Street in Berkeley. Then, after another year, when Jean and Artis had saved enough for a down payment on a house, we moved again, this time to Thermal Street in East Oakland.

During those two years, Jean and Artis had a child in 1961—my niece, Linda. I became her working uncle, by which I mean I was her nanny, a job I thoroughly enjoyed. When I was at school, I would take Linda to Aunt Elsie Luster Carter, my mother's sister, who lived in Oakland, to babysit her.

Sometimes, when I didn't have school, Jean would allow me to drive her and Artis's 1955 Chrysler after dropping her off at the hospital, to run errands for her. That's how I got to know the Oakland area.

Another responsibility I had was to prepare dinner—not every night, but occasionally. I cooked everything from fried chicken to black-eyed peas and cornbread.

Jean gave me a little spending money, and, starting when

I was still in high school, Aunt Gladys arranged for me to clean houses in the Oakland Hills and Piedmont, two wealthy neighborhoods, so I could earn a few bucks of my own. I toiled eight hours a day almost every Saturday, and occasionally on Sunday too, for a dollar an hour, working in White people's lovely homes with spectacular views of San Francisco Bay and the Golden Gate Bridge. After toiling in the sweltering cotton fields of Arkansas, I didn't mind scrubbing floors and doing general housecleaning. And I made eight dollars a day! I stashed seven, saving for the car that one day would take me across the bridge from Oakland to San Francisco.

My life during my first years in California didn't allow me much free time, but when it did I enjoyed reading and watching TV. I also liked to go to house parties. The biggest social gathering of that kind was hosted by Aunt Gladys, who was not to be outdone. She was the wily woman who had lured Jean away from Uncle Lemard and Pittsburg to the stylish charm of Oakland.

Aunt Gladys was a glamorous woman and a socialite in colored society. Every year between Christmas and New Year's, she would throw a party in her home in West Oakland, a nice two-story Victorian. At the foot of the large staircase just inside the front door, in a spot where the ceiling rose two floors, she would put the largest Christmas tree I ever saw.

Aunt Gladys was married to Charles LeGrand, a chef at the University of California at Berkeley, who would prepare exquisite food for her elegant Christmas parties. The guests would include dignitaries like Ron Dellums, who later became a long-serving congressman and ultimately the Mayor of Oakland.

At the first party I attended, when I was a senior in high school, Aunt Gladys invited me to clean up, paying me my usual rate of a dollar an hour. That would put five highly needed dollars into my pocket.

When I was in college, I was welcomed as a non-cleanup guest. Aunt Gladys and Uncle Charles were very supportive of my educational endeavors and would brag about me, "This is my nephew, Robert, who's in college!"

Whenever I had free time, my brother Leonard would drive out from Pittsburg to take me to my Uncle Lemard and Aunt Sybil's house. At that time, Leonard worked at the Mobil gas station on Railroad Avenue, which was owned by Uncle Lemard. Later, Leonard worked at the steel mill in Pittsburg.

When I arrived in California, Leonard already owned a car, a 1952 Chevrolet, which he had had professionally painted bright orange. It was a real showstopper. To ride around in that car meant we would immediately attract attention. He called the car "Little Egypt," which he had had professionally painted in bold letters on each side.

Occasionally, Leonard would let me drive Little Egypt. Whenever I had an important date, like escorting a girl to a prom, he would let me borrow it. I would take the bus out to Pittsburg and drive Little Egypt back down with me, then later return the car and take the bus back home to Jean's place. In those days, the drive from Oakland to Pittsburg took around half an hour. Today, it often takes two or three times longer to get through the traffic snarls.

All the members of my family were highly supportive of me, but no one made a big deal of my graduating from high school, which was fine with me. I didn't think the day was momentous or transformative, either. My focus was clearly on what came next—college.

I chose to get an early start at Merritt College by taking a summer course in English Literature. Since I had already excelled in English classes, I figured this would give me a chance to test my college preparedness. By the end of the session, I knew I was ready. But when I enrolled for a full course load in the fall, once again I failed to get the counseling I needed. What saved me is that I found my own personal guide, my cousin Fred Clement, whom I had met at church and discovered was attending the same college.

Fred was actually a second cousin. His mother, Eldora Harris Clement, and my father, Ben Harris, were first cousins. Fred was born in Gurdon, Arkansas, which is about twenty miles from Manchester. His family left for California when he was a baby, so he grew up in Oakland and had a lot of valuable information to share with me, the newcomer. In addition, Fred had been at Merritt for two years by the time I got there. That should have been enough for him to graduate, which made me worry if he might be on his way to becoming a professional student. But he said he intended to become an engineer, and ultimately he achieved his goal after transferring to UC Berkeley.

Fred tutored me on what would be required to transfer to a four-year college, making certain that I took the right courses to receive transfer credits at San Francisco State. When I registered at Merritt, I decided to major in sociology with the goal of becoming a probation officer or a social worker. Back at Oakland Tech, I had briefly thought of becoming a dentist. When someone asked me, "What would you like to be?" I immediately replied, "A dentist." But then I thought, *Why did I say that? Boring.*

Like so many others in the 1960s, I wanted to change society. As a probation officer, I believed, I could do that. So I enrolled in classes in sociology, psychology, and criminology, in addition to all the required courses that would lead to a smooth transfer to San Francisco State.

While I was in Merritt College, church continued to be important in my life. Fred and I attended Minglington Temple Church of God in Christ, in West Oakland, which is where we had met. We went to church for all the right reasons, but we were also both fascinated by a pair of sisters, the Clifton girls, who were the daughters of an assistant pastor of the church.

Fred was interested in the older sister, Carol, and I was interested in the younger one, Sonya. I really adored that girl. I would go to church early enough to make certain that I could get a good view of her and then try to talk to her. Sonya and I did go out on a couple of dates, but she clearly wasn't interested in me, for whatever reason. Fred, on the other hand, had a better relationship with Carol, and would occasionally invite me to go with him to her house. Figuring, as concerns Sonya, that where there's life, there's hope, I gladly tagged along. In the end, Fred lost Carol, but going to that house was a good experience for both of us because those sisters helped to keep us going to church.

In those early days at Merritt, although I did date a little, I was mostly focused on my studies, as well as saving money from my part-time work. I did make one friend at Merritt, Dale Rubin, who would influence my future career in a way I never imagined. Dale played football at Merritt and went on to play for Stanford. After he graduated from Stanford, he went to Boalt Hall, the law school at UC Berkeley, and was very instrumental in opening doors to other Black students, including me. He was a third-year law student when I enrolled as a first-year student.

Another friend I made at Merritt was Avon Manning, who had moved to California after graduating from high school in Mississippi. Avon was an interesting guy, who always seemed to be theorizing about something, while dramatically gesturing with his hands, almost like an orchestra conductor.

Like many of us, Avon worked at night—in his case, on the graveyard shift at the post office, from which he would come directly to class. On more than one occasion, Avon drifted off to sleep soon after class began. Nevertheless, he got his work done. In the end, we graduated from San Francisco State together, got our first jobs together, and became neighbors when we purchased our first homes.

9

Along Came Kappa Alpha Psi

*Every defeat, every heartbreak, every loss,
contains its own seed, its own lesson on how to
improve your performance the next time.*

—Malcolm X

It is difficult for some of us to pinpoint the exact moment when we make the leap from childhood to adulthood. There isn't always some dramatic life-changing event, one of those ah-ha moments when you know you'll never be the same again. Sometimes you can only discern the critical passage in retrospect.

I had never been reckless as a child, nor frivolous, nor lacking in direction. I almost thought I was born into maturity. But I was wrong. If I had to mark a time in my life when I became a man, it would be 1963 through 1964, when I had to overcome unexpected challenges.

In 1963, when I first entered San Francisco State, it had an enrollment of approximately 20,000 students, a daunting mass of people. I had never before been on a campus that large, which could have been a lonely experience for me, except that I often made the trip to and from school with friends.

We formed a carpool, taking turns behind the wheel for the one-hour-plus drive from Oakland to Lake Merced, where San Francisco State is located, on the western side of town. When it was my turn to drive, we rode dependably in my 1951 Chevrolet, whose transmission was in backwards, so I had to move the stick shift the opposite way than one would expect to keep us going in the right direction. I mastered that, thanks to the guidance of my brother-in-law, Artis, who was, after all, a teamster, who drove for a living. I had paid $150 cash for that car, and put it on Artis and Jean's insurance policy.

At San Francisco State, the classes were huge, and the teachers gave assignments without taking notice of any particular student. Roughly ten percent of the students were Black, which was highly unusual in those days for American colleges and universities. The library was very conducive to studying and easily accessible. However, there was a major distraction for the population of Black students: the cafeteria, known as The Commons. White students didn't spend much time there, and when they *were* there, they didn't mingle with the Black students. So The Commons was a part of campus that was seemingly dedicated to Black students.

From early in the morning until late at night, there was a serious game of Bid Wiz being played in The Commons. Some students got trapped there and didn't study because they were playing cards all day long rather than going to class or studying in the library. If you wanted to find a Black student on campus, you would go to The Commons and most likely either find that student or someone who knew exactly where he was. I played Bid Wiz occasionally, but mostly I studied when I wasn't working.

My best friend at San Francisco State was Lester MacDonald, whom I had gotten to know at Merritt College, but we became much closer at State. Lester was one of four siblings, with a sister and two brothers. He was a tall guy, good but not great at basketball, loved fishing, and majored in mathematics. His goal was to become a high-school teacher.

Lester and I often studied together, and he gave me the nickname "Skillroy" because I studied so hard. "If you want something done right," he would say, "give it to Skillroy."

When I had applied to State, I took a test with the other transferring students to determine my ability to articulate in the English language, use proper grammar, and show insight and analytical ability. Students who did not perform well on that test were required to take English 101, also called "Bonehead English," in their first semester after transferring. My performance on that essay exam gave my confidence a boost, not that it needed one. The test indicated that I would perform well on written examinations.

However, despite my confidence and the assurance of others in my academic potential, I did not do well in my first semester, thanks to pledging a fraternity. I was carrying a full load and working nights washing dishes at Herrick Hospital (later renamed Alta Bates) and cleaning houses on Saturdays, but I still wanted to join.

I had been exposed to fraternities at Merritt, but certain fraternities, including Kappa Alpha Psi, did not allow community college students to become members. Shortly after I started at State, I attended a few smokers, as the fraternity introduction parties were called. I went to the Phi Beta Sigma smoker as well as an Alpha Phi Alpha smoker and then a

Kappa Alpha Psi smoker. Lester MacDonald talked me into going to the Kappa smoker with him. Since it was the custom, alumni were present to persuade us that this or that was the best fraternity to join.

At the Kappa smoker, there was an impressive looking older man, Charles "Jack" Sudduth, who was part Native American, probably Cherokee, from Oklahoma. His ethnic blend gave him light skin, straight black hair, and unique imposing features. He exuded power and looked like he knew what he was doing.

"Jack," as he was called, was a well-known teacher and school administrator in the Bay Area, who had been one of the first Black school principals. From the moment I met him at the smoker, he was hugely impressive to me. I came away thinking, *If this organization produces this kind of person, maybe I should pledge.*

The guy also possessed a great sense of humor. One of his favorite lines was, "Every good Kappa man has a woman behind him, telling him he ain't worth a damn!"

Lester and I both decided to pledge Kappa, along with six other students. For four months, we had to prove that we had learned the history of the organization. Kappa Alpha Psi was founded on January 5, 1911, on the campus of Indiana University by ten men, known as the ten Founders. My fellow pledges and I learned a million details to prove that we had mastered the fraternity's history, traditions, customs, and songs. We also had to prove our willingness to take orders, however nonsensical, from our big brothers. Although we were pledges, that didn't guarantee we would be admitted to the membership. We needed a grade point average of 2.0 or better. We also needed the votes of two-thirds of the brothers.

The material requirements were one thing. The silly chores and the hazing were another. I wasn't happy with paddling, which reminded me of slavery, but my opinion carried no weight. Everyone who wanted to become a member of the fraternity had to go through the process. Pledging was about education, bonding, hazing, and being distracted from your studies.

The whole world seemed to be spinning so much faster in the fall of 1963. My university initiation, the fraternity, the parties, the coursework, the physical labor, and the driving were just the changes in my own immediate world. Beyond that, huge changes were under way in America. For one thing, after the successful March on Washington in August, there was renewed hope that the Kennedy administration would take federal action to enact civil rights laws. But so much of that hope was dampened on November 22, when an announcement blasted across the campus that President John F. Kennedy had been shot and killed in Dallas. It seemed as though every student froze in a moment of grief. And then there were the tears. Kennedy's victory over Richard Nixon in 1960 was the first national election in which I had a keen interest. The news of his death was so shocking—as if an asteroid had hit us.

At the same time, the semester was winding down, and I was headed for a huge personal shock. Because I was heavily engaged in pledge activities and not focusing on my studies, it shouldn't have been a surprise—although it was—that I ended up on academic probation with a GPA of 1.9. That was humiliating for me, first for having such a poor performance, and second for not meeting the academic requirement for initiation into Kappa. Lester was in the same boat, so we couldn't be initiated with the other six pledges. When those pledge brothers became our big brothers, that was especially demeaning.

That experience was a rude awakening for me. Because I had never performed so poorly in my academic life, my ego was bruised. One of my classes was statistics, a course that for non-math majors required time—which I had spent doing silly errands as a pledge. One of those errands required me to count the number of windows in the Wells Fargo Bank in downtown San Francisco. In addition to being hazed, we were expected to hang out. Although I hadn't hung out much at Merritt, and pretty much avoided the Bid Whiz games at State, there were parties I had to attend to become a Kappa.

The big brothers lived at a place known as Orizaba House, on Orizaba Street in San Francisco, which was a party haven for the fraternity. The Kappas and Kappa wannabes, as well as all the girls who wanted to date Kappas, were there every night of the weekend and often some weeknights.

I spent the spring semester recuperating from my academic disaster. In the end, that taught me a good lesson in setting priorities.

During that time, I met a Kappa named Tom Williams. I was at a wedding at Minglington Temple Church of God in Christ and was wearing the scroller pin worn by all the pledges of Kappa Alpha Psi. When Tom recognized me as a pledge because of my pin, we struck up a conversation. I soon learned that he was a pilot at the Alameda Naval Station. I found him very cordial in his presentation, and he soon became my big brother.

Having Tom as a big brother didn't mean constant harassment or meaningless chores. It meant spending time with someone I admired, who told me what life could be like. He encouraged me to stay focused on academic achievement, which motivated me at a low time in my life because of my academic probation. Tom gave me new perspective and a sense of direction, framing this period of my life as a setback rather than a failure—in other words, an opportunity to pursue new goals and objectives.

When Tom wasn't at the naval base, he spent a lot of time with me at Jean's house, talking with me about the fraternity, life in general, and academic achievement in particular. He helped me to draw distinctions between what was important and what was not, so that I could learn to focus on where I wanted to go. After being put on academic probation, I had begun to doubt whether I wanted to remain a pledge, but Tom convinced me that being a member of the fraternity was compatible with my goals for achievement. And he was right.

During our second semester as pledges, Lester and I focused on our studies and were initiated into Kappa Alpha Psi in the summer of 1964. Our initiation coincided with the national fraternity's Grand Conclave, which was held in San Francisco that year. Thus, at our initiation on July 18, 1964, one of the original ten Founders of the fraternity, Dr. Byron K. Armstrong, was present. Having one of the Founders there was a unique distinction, a fact that still fills me with pride.

Lester and I were immediately elected to positions of responsibility within our chapter, Gamma Alpha. Lester was elected Dean of Pledges, a position he enjoyed because he liked the idea of hazing, especially giving pledges silly errands to perform. I was elected Keeper of the Records, or secretary, a highly responsible position essential to good fraternity practices.

After I became a big brother, I did everything in my power to make certain that students were not unnecessarily distracted from their studies or hazed. I thought the proper emphasis should be on academics and achievements in the community. I was even responsible for getting a few fellow members suspended or expelled from the fraternity. Hazing and many other activities were not even allowed under our national fraternity rules, but everyone else tended to look the other way. I, on the other hand, reported everything I saw.

My leadership position in the Gamma Alpha chapter, which included San Francisco State, UC Berkeley, and surrounding colleges, was merely the beginning of my long history with my beloved fraternity.

The year that I was initiated, 1964, I met Ralph Grant, who pledged that year, after graduating from McClymonds High School in west Oakland. Ralph and I were friends for the next forty-five years. He was never in a sad mood, never frowned about anything, and was always smiling. Ralph majored in accounting at San Francisco State and later became a CPA. In fact, he was my accountant from the time I started my first job after graduation until he died in 2009.

To be around Ralph was inspiring. He had a "can do" attitude, never viewing anything as impossible. After a few years as a successful CPA, he went back to San Francisco State to get his MBA, and then to Golden Gate University to get a law degree and pass the California State Bar. He was so congenial in his approach that whenever I wanted good advice,

I went to Ralph, who could show me the positive side of just about anything.

As a graduate advisor to the Gamma Alpha chapter, I met John Burris while he was a student at Golden Gate University. He later became a well-known civil rights lawyer, who continues to be a good friend to this day. Back then, in 1966, he was a new initiate into the fraternity and was later elected Keeper of the Exchequer. John graduated from Golden Gate with a degree in accounting and, like Ralph, became a CPA, working for a while at one of the Big 8 firms. In 1970, when I was studying law at Boalt Hall, John was a year behind me, pursuing his own law degree plus an MBA.

With Elihu Harris (left) and John Burris

It was also through my membership in Kappa Alpha Psi that I met Elihu Harris (no relation) while he was at California State University, Hayward—now California State University, East Bay. I was the graduate advisor to the Gamma Alpha chapter when Elihu was in a group of eighteen pledges, but he stood out as a natural leader. His brilliance was obvious even then, as was his charisma. In his junior year, Elihu was elected student body president. Although he was born in California, he had family roots in Arkansas, like me. His father had attended Arkansas AM&N, at Pine Bluff, and his family then migrated to California, where they first settled in Oakland, and then moved to Berkeley, where they ran a funeral home.

When Elihu became Polemarch of Gamma Alpha, it was clear from the moment he was elected that he would make a real difference in the chapter. Under his leadership, the chapter became the largest in the fraternity. Elihu would later become a lawyer, a state Assemblyman, and the Mayor of Oakland, among many other distinguished positions in his career. He would also become a valued counselor to me in my various positions in national organizations.

I liked Elihu from the moment we met, because he was bright, articulate, and didn't hesitate to say what was on his mind. Almost immediately, he became my little brother, but I learned more from him than he learned from me. He was always inspirational and motivating, with good insights and great advice. What I liked most about him was that, like Ralph Grant, he had a "can-do" attitude. There was nothing he thought he couldn't achieve. In fact, we both fundamentally believed that we could make things happen.

Obviously, joining a fraternity in 1964 made a huge difference in my life, but something else happened during my first year at San Francisco State that had an equal impact.

In my senior year at Oakland Technical High, I had become friends with one of my classmates, Esther Metters, the daughter of a Baptist preacher who pastored Mt. Calvary

Missionary Baptist Church in Oakland. Esther was fairly reserved, musically inclined, and a very good student, who attended San Francisco State while I was still at Merritt College. Nevertheless, we maintained our friendship, and when I transferred to San Francisco State, we began dating and developed a very close and serious relationship. In early 1964, we got married while continuing on as students. Our son, Anthony Lester Harris, was born on November 3, 1964.

So, when I rang in the new year, 1965, I was off academic probation, working to support my family and to pay for my education, and enjoying being a member of a fraternity. Although my life had changed drastically, it was, once again, relatively stable. My goal—graduation—was within reach, and my career was about to begin.

10

Making a Difference

Every great dream begins with a dreamer. Always remember, you have within you the strength, the patience, and the passion to reach for the stars to change the world.

—Harriet Tubman

During my last year at San Francisco State, I was an intern at the Pacifica Police Department. Pacifica is a relatively small town that stretches for six miles along the Pacific coast just south of San Francisco. I worked from 4:00 to 8:00 P.M., accompanying police officers on patrol and watching them make stops and arrests. Part of my job was to learn all the police jargon and all the codes used to describe various operations.

The local newspaper covered my internship, perhaps because it was the first time the department had a Black intern. (Not too many Black people lived in Pacifica at that time.) I guess I impressed the chief, because when I graduated from college, he offered me a full-time job as an officer. Knowing that I wanted to help young men, particularly young Black men, rehabilitate themselves, rather than to arrest them, I turned the offer down.

That was 1965, the early days of the Black Power Movement and a pivotal moment in the Civil Rights Movement. Although the organized national struggle for civil rights had slowly but tirelessly been waged for more than fifty years, since the founding of the NAACP in 1909, the modern Civil Rights Movement had really intensified during the previous decade under the leadership of Dr. Martin Luther King, Jr.

In August 1963, Dr. King had given his "I Have a Dream" speech on the steps of the Lincoln Memorial before a crowd of 250,000 people. In response, President Kennedy promised civil rights legislation, and three months after his assassination, President Lyndon Johnson put his considerable legislative might behind a long and grueling congressional battle to pass the monumental Civil Rights Act of 1964 and the Voting Rights Act of 1965.

For the first time in their lives, the Black students at San Francisco State, the same ones who played Bid Wiz in The Commons, were seeing real concrete movement in civil rights. True, we were on an integrated campus, two thousand miles away from the Edmund Pettus Bridge in Selma, Alabama, and other sites of bloody protest in the South, but we understood the struggle to be *our* struggle as well, and that changing racial policies could impact our lives, too.

We were enormously influenced by Dr. King's strategy of nonviolence and passive resistance, but we were also deeply influenced by Malcolm X's call for the self-defense of our communities. That didn't necessarily mean arming ourselves. For some of us, at least, it meant taking responsibility for the changes we envisioned. There was much work to be done in the Black community—work that I began in my first job as a

Deputy Probation Officer in Alameda County.

Since Oakland is the county seat of Alameda County, it was home to me. When I was hired in June 1965, the county had one of its largest classes of Deputy Probation Officers ever—twenty-five men and women. Two of us were Black: Avon Manning, my good friend from college, and me. We started together one week after graduation.

At that time, I was twenty-one but looked nineteen, and I had a caseload of eighty juveniles. In those days, we were assigned a case immediately after the boy was arrested. Police officers brought the boys to the Juvenile Detention Facility, which was in our building, rather than to the city jail. After being given a case, I had to read the police report, interview the boy and all witnesses, and then make a determination about what to do. I had the power to dismiss the action or take it to court. My internship in the Pacifica Police Department paid dividends now, for I already knew the jargon.

If I took a case to court, a Juvenile Court judge would determine if there were sufficient evidence to proceed. If the boy were found responsible, he would be declared a ward of the court under Section 602 of the California Welfare and Institutions Code and placed under my supervision.

When I had to process a boy through the court procedures, I would have to file charges, write up the case, and then present it just as a lawyer would, indicating to the judge what the boy had allegedly done and why the court had jurisdiction. For all practical purposes, I essentially argued the case like a district attorney. The court would then base its determination on the evidence. In those days, a guilty boy was referred to as "responsible." He would then be placed on probation under my supervision if the court felt that he could be rehabilitated from home. If he were deemed a danger to society, he would be sent either to the Alameda County Boys' Camp, a lockup facility, or, if the case were more serious, the California Youth Authority.

If I determined that a case need not be brought to Juvenile Court, the boy might be placed on informal probation for a period of six months. This was typically done when the charges were minor. We would get an agreement from the parents to place their child on informal probation and avoid the court process altogether.

As a Deputy Probation Officer, I was expected to supervise the boy, which meant that I would visit his home, drop in at his school, and make certain that he was following the conditions of his probation, as set forth by the judge. I would meet with parents, teachers, and counselors, as well as with the boys one-on-one at the Probation Department office, which gave me a chance to provide guidance and mentorship. My being so young, 21, helped me to connect, and my being a college graduate with a good job made me a credible role model.

Many of the boys were in for car theft, usually joyriding. And then there were burglaries. There were very few juvenile homicides in the mid-1960s in Oakland; it wasn't at all common to see young people killing each other, as it is today. Charges also included battery and assault, related to fistfights that boys could be expected to get into. And occasionally there would be assault with a deadly weapon, where somebody had a knife and cut someone. There were very few gun-related incidents in those days. Drug-related offenses rarely occurred, and when they did, they usually involved marijuana. Gang-related activity was not something I had to deal with, because there were few, if any, gangs back then.

What I am attempting to show is that boys were not treated like criminals at that time. After they were arrested, their cases were not turned over to an Assistant District Attorney, as they are today. Rather, as I pointed out, they came to us first, and Deputy Probation Officers could serve such multiple functions because the proceedings were non-adversarial. The entire legal system was designed to act in the best interests of the boys.

Our goal was not to extract punishment—as it is today—but to rehabilitate. (There were, of course, young girls processed through the Juvenile Court system, but female probation officers supervised and mentored them.) As a young Black man, I found it particularly rewarding to have a chance to lead those boys to the right track. If they didn't violate any terms of their probation for six months, they would never have to go before the court. I would say that happened in about ninety percent of the cases. Only about ten percent were repeat offenders. However, the U.S. Supreme Court's decision in 1970, requiring juveniles to be subject to the same standard of proof as adults, ended the non-adversarial practices of the Juvenile Court, thus bringing prosecutors onto the scene.

From my visits to the schools to check if the boys were truant, I discovered that most of those under my supervision were registered for the bonehead classes that I, with Artis and Jean's help, had managed to avoid. They were taking courses that could not possibly hold their attention or provide them with a vision for their future. I had avoided injury from low expectations, but these boys were fulfilling the path that had been predicted for them. They were considered disciplinary problems at school long before they committed the acts that put them in the juvenile system. So, an important part of my mentoring was to convince those boys that they could do more than what some people in and out of school thought they were capable of.

I worked Monday through Friday from 8:00 A.M. to 6:00 P.M. for a starting salary of five hundred dollars per month, which was a lot of money in those days. After six months, I had my own office, and my salary increased by fifty dollars per month. I thought I was living high on the hog. My career was under way. I also remained active in Kappa Alpha Psi, mainly through the Berkeley alumni chapter, which is where I met James L. Bradford, or "Brad."

Brad's title was Keeper of Records, or secretary, a position he used to wield a great deal of power. Beyond being keeper of all the paper records, he was known within the chapter as the gatekeeper. He could either make or break you. Everyone learned that if you wanted "things to go right," you needed to be on the good side of Brad. And I was. We became close friends. He was a father figure for me, offering guidance and supervision in the land of Kappa Alpha Psi.

What impressed me most about Brad was his organizational ability, especially his talent for remembering information and keeping meticulous records, which set him apart from the rest of us. There wasn't a single question about the chapter that he couldn't answer. He had access to every conceivable fact in his mind—and if he didn't, it would be in a file at his fingertips in just a few minutes. Today, with computers, keeping records is so much easier. In those days, the votes on various issues, the number of members over the years, and other similar matters made his skills really essential and impressive. He was a living example of the saying, "Knowledge Is Power!"

Brad and his wife, Margaret, lived in Berkeley on Hearst Avenue. Later, when I attended law school in Berkeley, I would often stop by their house on my way home. I enjoyed chatting with Brad because he was a great listener, and there were times when I really needed to unload. As I pursued my educational objectives, he encouraged me to stay focused. Brad had a master's degree in education and was one of the few Black elementary school principals in the Bay Area at that time. He had a deep commitment to family, fraternity, and community, all of which rubbed off on me.

Another person who took me under his wing at the time was Charles "Jack" Sudduth, whom I had actually met at San Francisco State when I attended my first Kappa event. Jack had now risen to the rank of Province Polemarch within the fraternity—that is, president of a region. Like Brad, he gave me the drive and inspiration at various stages to move up to the next level. At each stage, I worked hard and took nothing for granted. I didn't seek to move to any particular position or office. I simply did everything in the present moment, with the intent to do my best. Brad and Jack pushed me in my advancement in Kappa Alpha Psi, an ascent that one day would take me to the very top of the fraternity as its Grand Polemarch (national president).

So, I really had two godfathers at the time, although I still had a real Daddy, whom I continued to rely on. From time to time, I made phone calls back to Arkansas to have my personal preacher pray for me. He never hesitated to give me those words of inspiration that I needed to move forward.

*Pinned by the Outgoing Grand Polemarch, Ulysses McBride,
as the 27th Grand Polemarch*

As I pointed out earlier, I was one of two Black males hired in the 1965 class of twenty-five new probation officers. After Avon Manning and I completed our training, Dennis Handis, another Black recruit, joined us in the department. Dennis, who was also a Kappa Alpha Psi brother from San Francisco State, had majored in biology with dreams of becoming a doctor. Instead, he distinguished himself in probation. First, he moved up the ladder in the Alameda County Probation Department, and then became the Chief Probation Officer of Santa Clara County, before ending up as the Chief Probation Officer of San Joaquin County. He was the first Black chief in both counties, quite a distinction in Northern California.

George Holland and Carl Morris were two other Black colleagues at the Probation Department who have remained longtime friends. Both of them had graduated from San

Francisco State and then worked as bank tellers. We had crossed paths in college, but we weren't close then. George and Carl attended Golden Gate University Law School at night while working as probation officers, determined to become lawyers. One other Black colleague, Tom Broome, who planned to become a lawyer, was attending San Francisco Law School.

All three of these associates became successful lawyers. Carl retired as an Alameda County Superior Court Judge. George became president of the California Association of Black Lawyers and a longtime president of the Oakland Branch of the NAACP. And Tom became a noted criminal trial lawyer and the president of the National Bar Association.

The seed for the idea of becoming a lawyer was planted in my mind by their examples, although I couldn't see myself following in their night-law-school footsteps. With a family and a full-time job, I didn't see going to law school as a viable option.

While we were still young probation officers, Avon, Carl, Dennis, Tom, George, and I, along with some others, established an organization called Counseliers West, whose objective was to provide support for Black probation officers. I am not suggesting that there was a pressing need for our group. There was no overt racial discrimination that I recall during the years I spent in the department. Rather, our group was more of a collegial forum. I also belonged to a larger organization of probation officers that was mostly White.

With fulfilling work and steady pay raises, I felt that my life was going well. Around 1968, my wife and I purchased our first home—a townhouse in Richmond, a small city twenty miles northwest of Oakland. We had two children then: in addition to Anthony Lester "Tony" Harris, Regina Carol Harris was born on March 27, 1966.

Also in 1968, my co-worker and friend, Avon Manning, purchased a house in Richmond with his wife, about a block away, in the Laurel Park development. We were so close that we even bought a lawnmower together, which passed back and forth between the two houses without a problem. At that point, I was expecting to spend the rest of my working life in the Alameda County Probation Department.

That wasn't going to happen.

11

Assassination

Faith is taking the first step even when you don't see the whole staircase.

—Dr. Martin Luther King, Jr.

On April 4, 1968, I left the home of one of the boys in my charge in East Oakland. When I got into my car and turned on the radio, I heard a news announcement that was so shocking that I literally froze in disbelief. Dr. King had been shot and killed in Memphis.

I sat there with the engine running because I just couldn't move. I don't know how long I was there, but it was a while. That night and in the seething nights that followed, riots broke out across the nation—in Baltimore, Washington, Louisville, Kansas City, Chicago, Los Angeles, and other urban Black communities. Oakland erupted too, but not nearly to the degree of those other cities. A combination of anger and fear gripped many Americans. Tragedy had led to more tragedy. Would we descend into civil war? What good could come of the murder of a man of peace?

What I could not see at the time, and what many Black

Americans could not immediately see, was that Dr. King's assassination might be a turning point. I wondered, *How long?* And the answer came back to me: *Too long.* Something had to change. In the wake of the assassination and the rioting, there was an acknowledgment by some influential White journalists, politicians, academics, and church leaders that huge racial disparities existed in America. Clearly, affirmative action was needed to improve race relations. That change in attitude would redirect the course of my life.

Boalt Hall, the distinguished law school at the University of California at Berkeley, decided to actively recruit Black students. Prior to 1968, Boalt Hall had only admitted two or three Blacks a year, although some classes didn't have any Blacks at all. That was the situation despite the fact that Boalt Hall had had some outstanding Black students who would distinguish themselves in their legal careers—people like Don Warden, who became a highly successful lawyer and lecturer; Henry Ramsey, who ultimately became a professor at Boalt Hall, a Dean of the Howard University Law School, and an Alameda County Superior Court judge; Clinton Wayne White, who became a famous trial lawyer and was appointed to the California Court of Appeals; Thelton Henderson, who became a distinguished U.S. District Court judge in San Francisco; and Allen Broussard, who became the second Black justice on the California Supreme Court.

That Boalt Hall was now interested in increasing the number of Black students was never publicly advertised. That fact came to me by word-of-mouth from a White colleague in the probation department, Dennis MacDonald. Like three of my Black colleagues, Dennis was attending law school at night. I had never given serious consideration to the idea of attending law school until the moment Dennis said, "I think you should apply."

I thought it through thoroughly. What skills did I have that would be relevant to success in law school and in legal practice? First, writing. Around that time, Avon Manning and I had enrolled in a part-time graduate program in Public Administration at California State University, Hayward. I did all the reading and writing assignments for Public Administration 101, and received an *A* in the class.

The truth is, I had always enjoyed and performed well in courses that required a lot of reading and writing, such as those in literature and history, two of my favorite subjects. Additionally, my work in the probation department gave me experience in writing legal documents and presenting oral arguments before a judge. My investigative reports were highly detailed—in fact, they were known for being a bit flowery at times—so I had developed a reputation as an effective representative for the boys under my supervision.

When I sought the advice of my family, since I knew I would need their support, no one said, "That's a crazy idea!" Everyone was one hundred percent behind me. So, I began the process, first taking the nationally standardized Law School Admissions Test (LSAT). I wrote out the application, attached my transcripts from college, and obtained a recommendation from one of the judges who frequently presided in Juvenile Court, Judge Robert Barber.

Because I had no intention of relocating, given that I had a young family, and couldn't see upending the stable life we enjoyed, I only applied to one law school: Boalt Hall. Besides,

I didn't know if other law schools were also intent on admitting more Black students. I viewed going to Boalt Hall as a great opportunity that had come my way by chance. It was certainly worth giving it a try, come what may.

The next question was: *If I get in, can I afford it?*

My wife was an elementary-school teacher, so we had her salary. I also had some savings and access to a retirement fund through my job, which I could draw upon. If I went to Boalt Hall, I would have to attend full-time because the school didn't have a part-time program. The tuition, $750 per semester, was financially feasible.

In a letter I received in early April 1969, I learned that I had been accepted!

The class that entered Boalt Hall in the fall semester of 1969 had 330 students, of whom ten were Black. Of those ten, three were women. Two of the ten dropped out for unknown reasons during the first year, including one of the women. Eight of us made it to graduation in the Class of 1972.

Throughout my academic life—from my early education in Arkadelphia to my graduation from San Francisco State, plus the one graduate course I had taken—I had been hard-working. The embarrassing result of that first semester at San Francisco State while pledging Kappa Alpha Psi was the only painful blemish in my academic career. Still, despite that track record for intellectual seriousness, I found that law school was a different animal.

The other Black students and I faced our own formidable challenges. I had been accepted even though my LSAT score was not high, and I had not graduated from an elite undergraduate institution with stellar grades. Affirmative action had gotten me and my Black classmates in the door. The faculty knew that and, I think, they had low expectations that we would be able to meet the academic standards of the law school. But they expected us to compete from day one; and, honestly, we didn't expect, nor were we given, special treatment. If our professors were supportive, it was no more so than the courtesy and support they extended to White students.

My goal was certainly not to be at the top of my class. Before law school, I had not been at the top of my class. I had always been decidedly above average or near the top, but I had never been able to give my studies my full attention because, beginning with picking cotton, I had always worked while in school. So be it. I believed that the purpose of school was not to end up at the top of the class, but rather to learn certain concepts and to be educated to a sufficient degree that I could apply the knowledge in my work. Success in school was about being able to demonstrate a competitive level of proficiency with the material when the time came, either on exams or in the real world. The endgame was what I would achieve in the real world. Law school was only the foundation on which to develop legal skills needed to be a competent lawyer.

Prior to entering law school, I had discovered that there was a program to prepare students like me, offered by the Council on Legal Educational Opportunities, or CLEO for short. The course provided a preview on briefing cases, recognizing issues, and understanding the law. I had found out about CLEO's summer program after receiving my acceptance letter from Boalt. So, my options were (a) to resign from the probation department before the summer and take the thousand-dollar scholarship offered by the CLEO Program, or

(b) to work for an additional three months during the summer in the probation department, where I was earning more than that a month.

I had to consider all the anticipated expenses of attending law school, not least of which would be for books. The average cost of a law school text in those days was around fifty dollars. A first year's worth of required texts would amount to roughly three hundred dollars, a lot of money in those days when gas only cost a quarter a gallon. So, I decided that I needed to stay in the probation department as long as I could.

12

A New Journey

*Education is our passport to the future, for tomorrow
belongs to the people who prepare for it today.*

—Malcolm X

Most of my studying was done either in the Boalt law
library after class until 6:00 or 7:00 P.M., and then I would
continue at home until about 11:00. The next morning, I was
up early and back at school before 7:00. By getting to the law
school early, I was usually able to find free parking on the
street near the campus because I drove a small British import,
a Morris Minor, so I could squeeze into spaces that larger cars
had to pass by.

The first-year curriculum required the standard courses
that every beginning law student takes: Contracts, Torts,
Property, Criminal Law, Evidence, and Civil Procedure. My
first semester was intense, strange, and much more demanding
than what I had ever experienced academically before. I was
in a class of uniformly bright students, so the competition was
keen. It's one thing to be hopeful of success, and quite another
to be concretely sure of it.

Ever since the days of reciting the Bible book titles at the age of six, my academic confidence had been rooted in my ability to read and memorize facts and details. The first class I attended was a Torts course that dealt with personal injuries. As I saw it, all I needed to do was read the cases, memorize the facts, and explain why the courts had reached their decisions. Rather easy, I thought.

To my surprise, understanding the facts of a case and explaining a court's decision were merely the entrance fees. The professor seemingly could not have cared less about those aspects. He was more interested in challenging our critical thinking skills. I quickly learned that, in major law schools, professors use what is called the Socratic Method of teaching, which is designed to intimidate students by determining whether they really understand the fundamental concepts of a case and why a court's ruling may or may not rest on solid principles. That was disconcerting, to say the least. After being pounced on by the professor two or three times, I was certain that there was no "correct" answer to *any* question.

Like everyone else, I was assigned to a small study section of approximately twenty students to practice the Socratic Method in a friendlier environment. I needed that. Every week, the professor gave us a practice exam that provided us with a fact-filled scenario that required a legal resolution. Those exams gave us opportunities to apply the basic principles that we had learned about the legal subject under consideration. Gradually, with increasing success, I discovered that the law is not a science, but an art.

At the end of the first semester, we had final exams in early January, right after we returned from the holidays. I did well enough to shed all my doubts about success, and began appreciating Socratic questioning as a learning tool. I began to see that it was designed to equip future lawyers with the ability to question themselves and others about what they know and don't know, and whether their conclusions can withstand critical analysis. That was a revelation that was later to prove quite helpful to me as a practicing lawyer and leader of various organizations.

The second semester of my first year went pretty much the same way as the first one, only more so. I learned more about how to study law and how to participate in class. I also began to learn more about my classmates, and made several long-lasting friends.

Lockers were assigned alphabetically, so Jimmie Harris had been assigned a locker next to mine. We weren't related, but we were both members of Kappa Alpha Psi—fraternity brothers—and quickly became friends. Jimmie had come directly from college, and so he was four years younger than I. His undergraduate education at the University of Illinois, where he had majored in engineering, had prepared him very well for Boalt Hall. Engineers are highly analytical, an orientation that is well suited for a career in law. Jimmie's arrogance may have turned some people off, but that didn't hurt him. He was everything he thought he was. I never once beat him on a test.

Another friend I made that first year was a really colorful character by the name of Reggie Brown. He drove a two-seater convertible Jaguar, a very expensive car. Reggie always had something going on. He bet on the races and even owned a racehorse. He also took money from fellow law students to place bets on races for them. Clearly, he was not as focused as one should have been on legal studies. However, he graduated, passed the bar exam, and became a practicing attorney.

Another acquaintance of mine in law school was Calvin Grigsby, also a member of Kappa Alpha Psi. Calvin was quite a character, too. He seemed to be happy most of the time, as if he were smoking something. Born in Arkansas, like me, he came out of Arizona State University and was wild-looking, with a huge unruly Afro. You never knew what Calvin was doing or what he was about to do, but he was a very bright young man. Like Reggie, he was a fan of shortcuts, but was known for always doing well, despite preparing at the last minute. After graduating, he passed the bar exam and landed a job at a major law firm. Five years later, however, he switched careers to investment banking, where he did very well.

After we completed the first year of law school, Calvin, Jimmie, and I were invited to be members of the Law Review. It was unprecedented for three Black students to be selected at the same time. The year before, two Black students had made it, so for one overlapping year, there were five of us on Law Review out of approximately sixty students. We spent our time doing research and getting ready to publish. In fact, it was on Law Review that I finally beat Jimmie at something. As members of the Law Review, we were expected to publish at least one article in the journal. Despite Jimmie's knack for procrastination, he did end up publishing the one article required. However, I published *two*.

During the summer between my first and second year, I returned to the Alameda County Probation Department to work for $1,000 per month. The job was more lucrative than most legal internships I might have obtained, and I appreciated being invited to return.

When the second year started, I was no longer frightened. While many of my classmates were complaining about how burdensome their courses were, I was a bit cocky. The difference was that I simply enjoyed studying and spent a lot of time at it. I convinced myself that it was better to prepare myself then than to wait till I was practicing. I wanted to be equipped to deal with the issues that were likely to come up in my career.

Unlike some other students, I didn't consider working on the Law Review a waste of time. Rather, I viewed it as an exciting learning opportunity, and it was certainly prestigious to have been selected. My first published article was on juvenile law, and the second one was on the arcane second-degree felony murder rule in California. By the end of my second year, it was time to seriously consider where I wanted to work after graduation and to set up an internship before my third and final year.

After several interviews, I was fortunate to be selected by a respected San Francisco law firm, Howard Rice, which had thirty-five attorneys. That summer, I commuted by AC Transit bus from Richmond to San Francisco, where I worked from 8:00 A.M. to 5:00 P.M., doing research and writing legal memoranda. The internship paid $1,000 per month, excellent wages for a law clerk at the time.

13

Praying for the Bar Exam

Heavenly Father, be with us.

—Daddy

The California Bar Exam rattles everyone who takes it. Only about half of the applicants pass. Back then, it certainly rattled the few Black law students who were matriculating through various law schools. There was a widespread belief that "only so many, if any" of us would be allowed to pass on our first try. Black applicants to the bar would go so far as to say, "They have your number," a belief that became many an applicant's nemesis.

I refused to believe that bar graders would automatically flunk applicants when they identified them as Black. I knew that when you received a copy of your answer, which you had the right to request if you failed, you could make the case to the legal community that your answer deserved a passing score.

I studied for the bar exam with Jimmie Harris and Andrew Owens, another Black law school graduate from the University of San Francisco. My preparation was psychological as well as analytical. Studying for that exam was one of the most rigorous exercises in my life, so I was determined to go through that agony only once. We spent the appropriate amount of time studying, going over past exams, drafting practice answers, and reviewing each other's essays. In fact, we did everything that would be expected of students preparing for the bar exam, including taking a bar preparation course. We set a rigorous study schedule and convinced ourselves that we were going to pass.

Whenever I needed to mentally overcome the low expectations that I feared others had of me, I remembered the encouraging words of my parents, my teachers in segregated schools, and all the other motivating persons in my life who told me I would be somebody. After my encounter with Mrs. Hillegas, the Oakland Tech counselor who didn't believe I would perform well in college prep classes, I was thoroughly convinced that if someone told me I couldn't do something, it meant that I *could*. Many of us become dejected when someone tells us that we cannot do something. Some people believe it when others tell them that it isn't in the cards for them. They become demoralized, embittered, and give up. For me, discouragement is an indication that I can do something.

I told myself that I had complete control over whether or not I passed. No one had that control but me. Therefore, I did what was necessary physically and psychologically to prepare. No one had *my* number. I planned to write an exam that I would be proud to show to the world.

Two days before I was scheduled to take the bar exam, I felt that I had done as much studying as humanly possible, but was still missing an essential ingredient. Thus, on Sunday evening, I telephoned Mother to tell her that I had spent the past several weeks preparing night and day for the exam, and that I really wanted to pass it and not have to take it again.

After listening to me politely, she said, "Robert Lewis, you are going to pass the exam because you are smart."

Conceding that I was prepared, I said, "I think I need something more."

"I'm going to ask Ben [Daddy] to pray for you to pass the exam," she said.

Although I had been raised in the church, I had not been as faithful as I should have been after moving to California, but facing the daunting challenge of the bar exam in a couple of days, I believed that having Daddy pray for me was a great idea.

Mother called him to the phone, and after she spoke to him for a moment, he began his prayer—as he always did—with the words, "Heavenly Father, be with us as we call on you."

He followed that with a request to Jesus to enter the exam room and guide me as I undertook the rigors of the test. While I do not recall all of his exact words, I do remember that he prayed for about five minutes, which seemed to me like forever. I kept my eyes closed while he spoke. For the first time since I had left Arkansas, twelve years earlier, I really believed that divine intervention was with me and could accompany me into the bar exam. Now I *knew* I would pass.

When the time came to take the test, Jimmie and I had been assigned to the same test center at the Hastings College of Law in San Francisco, so we stayed at a nearby hotel in order to avoid having to drive across the Bay Bridge on the three mornings of the exam.

We had been forewarned that, at lunch during the first day

of the exam, people tended to congregate in Hastings' cafeteria to talk about issues they had spotted.

"Did you get that point about the rule against perpetuities?"

"Did you see that trick issue about tort liability?"

If we participated in those discussions, we would spend the balance of the first day thinking about the morning session of the exam, recalling what we may have missed, so Jimmie and I had agreed to talk exclusively with each other during lunch.

The California Bar Exam required us to write essays for two whole days, and then answer multiple choice questions on general law during the morning of the third day. When I took the exam in 1972, it was the first time the multiple choice section counted toward whether or not you passed. I felt that this section held the most promise for its certainty: you either knew the correct answer, or you didn't. As the exam unfolded, I became more and more confident with each question that I would pass. Because we had reviewed so many past exams, the issues, and even some factual scenarios, were familiar. There were variations, but nothing was completely new.

When the exam was over, I felt so confident that I said to Jimmie, "If I didn't pass *this* exam, I don't know if I could *ever* pass the bar exam."

We took that exam at the end of July, and the results wouldn't come out till mid-November. Although I was fairly certain I had passed, my confidence did not eliminate the anxiety I experienced during those four months of waiting for the actual results.

In the meantime, getting employed as a lawyer was my immediate challenge. My previous summer job at Howard Rice led to nothing. I had worked on good assignments, including a copyright case about the "Peanuts" comic strip by Charles Schulz. I had spent considerable time doing research, and had learned a lot about copyright law as a result. But I felt that I had essentially wasted a summer, since I didn't have a job offer at the end of the internship. The only good news was that neither of the other two interns who served with me, both of them White, were offered a job, either.

During my third year of law school, I had interviewed with every major law firm in San Francisco, but despite being a member of the Law Review and having had a noteworthy internship, I did not receive an offer from any of the firms. The trouble was that I had a young family, and time was ticking. I wondered what I was going to do.

Jimmie had received an offer from a prestigious law firm in Los Angeles, but I had intentionally restricted my search to the Bay Area, not wanting to uproot my family. I had interviewed with the Alameda County Legal Services Agency, and had received an offer from them, but that was not the path I envisioned for myself. I wanted to work in a law firm or for a major corporation. I had every intention of giving back to the community, but I simply had that vision for myself at that time.

Fortunately, while I was reluctantly thinking of accepting the Legal Aid offer, the director of the placement office at Boalt Hall gave me a lead for a job opening at Pacific Gas and Electric.

Yes, I was interested!

She arranged for the interview.

14

The Battle of Berkeley

*The world is before you and you need not take it or
leave it as it was when you came in.*

—James Baldwin

Within a few days, I was at 77 Beale Street in San Francisco
on the thirty-first floor. Pacific Gas and Electric, or PG&E for
short, is a Fortune 500 company, one of the largest gas and
electricity utilities in the country, serving California customers
from Bakersfield to the Oregon border. When the job opening
was presented to me, I didn't even know that PG&E had its
own legal department with a staff of two dozen lawyers. That
was impressive.

My first meeting was with a man named Brad Bunning. He
was a most cordial young lawyer, very engaging, and seemed
interested in having me come aboard. The interview went well,
but having already gone through this process with so many
law firms, I remained guarded. However, when Brad invited
me back, my hopes were raised.

This was different from all my other interviews because it
was the first time I was invited to a second round of questioning.

I met with more people, all of whom seemed to like me. But during the hiring process, I had to go through all kinds of scrutiny because—as I learned later—a Black man newly hired to the department a year before, who was a graduate of Boalt, had failed to pass the bar exam on his first try. He had to be let go, which was a disappointment to everyone.

This young man had been the third Black attorney hired by PG&E. The first one was Don Mitchell, who had been employed four years earlier. His two years at PG&E had been uneventful, but he was hired away to be legal counsel for the Boise Cascade Company. The second Black man hired was a fellow named Burt Golden, who was reportedly at PG&E for only several months, but then left for personal reasons. In those days, companies didn't hire more than one Black at a time, and they wanted that token lawyer to succeed.

So, I was asked to produce nearly every piece of paper possible to convince the committee making the hiring decision that I was likely to pass the bar exam on my first try. They wanted to read the two articles I had written for the Law Review, and they also asked me to submit my transcripts and other papers I had written for classes. While I had no objections, it was unusual at the time to be asked to submit those materials. I knew that because my law school colleagues and I compared notes about our job searches, and one of them, Dennis Sullivan, who was a White student in my class, had been hired a few months ahead of me at PG&E without being required to submit those materials.

I was even asked to provide my law school admissions test score. I could have stood on principle by questioning such scrutiny, but I was not about to do that. I wanted the job. I understood the company's desire to avoid the embarrassment of having two Black hires in a row fail the bar exam, so I accepted the burden of having to prove that I was likely to pass.

They explained to me, in no uncertain terms, that if they hired me, I could work as a law clerk while I waited for the bar exam results, but when those come out, I had to pass, or I would have to leave my job immediately. So, that was the condition under which I took the job. I started on September 15, 1972, knowing full well that if I didn't pass the bar exam, I would be out of the job the very next day.

Three people were hired by the legal department that year: one White man (Dennis Sullivan); one White woman (Kathy Todrank), the first female lawyer ever to be hired by PG&E; and one Black man—me. The same first-attempt requirement applied to the others.

The offices at 77 Beale Street in the Financial District of San Francisco, the corporate headquarters of PG&E, were impressive. The building had just opened in 1971, the year before I arrived. There were thirty-two floors, with the executive suites at the top and the legal department just below that. On my first day, I was assigned an office right near an entrance door to my department.

It was a nice office, a good size, but windowless, so I had to keep the door open for air circulation. As soon as a visitor opened the door to the legal department, the first office he would see was mine. And the visitor was likely to see me, a brown-skinned man with a neatly coiffed Afro. That reminded me of the title of a very popular book that had been published in 1969: *The Spook Who Sat by the Door* by Sam Greenlee.

The title referred to a practice at the time whereby token Blacks were hired to fill very visible positions in companies that were keen on displaying an integrated staff.

There were twenty-four lawyers, all White men, in the legal department, plus three law clerks, as we three new hires were known until we received notice that we had passed the bar exam and were sworn in. The general counsel at the time was Fred Searles, who stood about six feet tall, looked distinguished, and had a gentlemanly demeanor. He made us feel comfortable in his presence and under his leadership.

My first assignment was to assist a lawyer who had been one of my interviewers, Richard "Dick" Clarke, who was a senior counsel at the time. Like Fred, Dick was impressive in stature and demeanor. He looked the type. If Hollywood had been casting for the perfect lawyer-looking actor, Dick would have been the model. He had graduated from Boalt Hall and had worked at PG&E for ten years, left for private practice for five years, and then returned and had been working in the legal department for a few more years before I was hired. He was known for being very scholarly and demanding.

Within the first few days of my arrival, I had lunch with a group of lawyers from the department.

One of them said to me, "Do you know you're the only person working for Dick Clarke?"

Is there anything wrong with that? I thought.

He continued, "Do you know why no one else will work for him?"

"I have no idea."

So, he and the others proceeded to tell me about Dick's reputation. Dick was nicknamed King Richard after the bloody dictator of Shakespeare's play *Richard III*. Nobody could work with Dick, they said. Nobody could please him. Anyone who was assigned to him would be decimated within a few days, or a few weeks at most, and Dick would get rid of them. They wouldn't be fired, but they would work for someone else in the legal department, and never work for King Richard again.

So, I left that lunch a bit concerned that I had been assigned to work for someone with such an intimidating reputation.

Am I being set up for failure?

After my first two or three legal research assignments for Dick, whatever fear I had soon dissipated. He would critique my writing, always finding fault, and would offer a different perspective. To say he was supercritical would be an understatement, but it sharpened my analytical skills. It wasn't long before word got around: Dick Clarke could work with Bob Harris. That clearly was a plus, but until the bar exam results came out, I still had a big question mark hanging over my head.

Rumor had it that the results would arrive by mail in a big envelope if you failed, and in a small envelope if you passed.

One day, in late November, I was standing on my lawn with Avon Manning and another neighbor, Henry Fort, who both knew I was waiting for the results of the bar exam. We were standing there talking when the mailman pulled up.

One of my friends said, "I hear the bar exam results are coming out today."

When I saw that the mailman had a large brown envelope, I thought, *I flunked! How could that happen?*

Momentarily frozen by fear, I hesitated for a second before I opened the envelope and scanned the letter. The first word I saw was *Congratulations*. The rest was a blur. I saw nothing but that one word. I didn't open any of the other papers. I knew they wouldn't congratulate me if I hadn't passed. The wait was over.

I rushed into the house to tell Esther, and then I called just about everybody I knew. That night, we had a celebratory dinner. It was a Saturday, and I was congratulated the next day at a fraternity meeting. On Monday, the legal department exploded in excitement because all three new hires had passed the bar exam. The whole department went out to lunch.

I was sworn in on December 13, 1972, as a member of the Bar of the State of California. My mother, who hadn't gotten beyond elementary school, came out on a Greyhound bus from rural Arkadelphia to witness my achievement, which was very much her achievement, too. She was the one who had shown me that I could retain vast amounts of information, and, when put under pressure, I could display that knowledge.

Being admitted to the bar was exciting, but the enormity of my long journey really struck me the following day. As I sat in an elegant PG&E conference room with my boss, Dick, and several other executives, I couldn't help wondering how a Black country boy, who had grown up surrounded by the cotton fields of Arkansas, could be sitting here, surrounded by these older White men.

How do I fit in this picture?

Many such thoughts rushed through my mind.

Am I going to survive in this Fortune 500 company?

It was nerve-wracking; it was exciting; it was surreal.

The meeting was a strategy session. The group was preparing for a "dog and pony" show to explain why it didn't make good economic sense for cities and towns in the PG&E service area to take over the electric facilities of PG&E via eminent domain, and then operate those facilities themselves as a means of generating revenue. Getting ready for a three-day trip to the northern part of PG&E's service territory, the group of seven, including me, was mapping out a complex strategy to convince various audiences that PG&E was the most capable entity to provide electric service to their jurisdictions at the best price.

With Dick Clarke, Chairman and CEO of PG&E

My inclusion as the youngest member of the team caused some tension in the legal department because one of the senior lawyers, who had formerly been a member of the team, had been replaced by me, a brand new lawyer with no experience. That seemed a bit unusual to me, but I was merely following the assignment given to me by Dick, who was the head of the team. The removed lawyer wanted very much to remain on the team because of the high visibility of an election that would be required by law to seek condemnation of the company's electric facilities. I understood his disappointment and resentment. After all, what did *I* know about the concept of eminent domain as it relates to public utilities? Confident person that I am, I was still uncomfortable. I felt like an alien in a strange land. Why had I been chosen for this assignment? I had to catch up, and so I read everything I could find on the matter to get up to speed quickly! It was a challenge.

By the time we completed our tour of the northern service territory, I could see a little light at the end of the tunnel, as I began to understand the complicated evaluation process for determining the market value of an electric system when subjected to an eminent domain proceeding. Since such a situation is rare, it involves extensive analysis and speculation about market value. In this case, there was little, if any, market data about value and other factors by which a court could determine fair compensation for a condemned electric facility.

I was truly amazed and impressed by all the reasons that PG&E had developed to convince voters that while it made sense for PG&E to operate electric systems, it made absolutely no sense for a government entity to operate such facilities. It was an intriguing argument that provided the very foundation for PG&E to retain its reign over its electric facilities. Within two weeks, thanks to Dick, I became an accepted member of the "dog and pony" team.

Still, I wondered, *Why me? Why this young, Black, inexperienced lawyer on this highly technical team of White boys?*

I soon figured it out.

The next month, January 1973, the City of Berkeley, often

referred to as the "People's Republic of Berkeley," announced its intention to pass a ballot measure to take over the electric system of PG&E within its city limits and operate it itself. Having attended UC Berkeley's law school, I was thoroughly familiar with the many controversial issues that came before the Berkeley City Council, one of the most radical city councils in the nation, which opposed, among other things, the Vietnam War.

With much media attention, the campaign to convince Berkeley voters to take over PG&E's electric facilities was met with enthusiasm, especially by left-leaning groups. As a large monopoly, PG&E started with a decided disadvantage in the radical city.

The election was set for April 17, 1973. The ballot proposition, Measure 8, if passed by voters, would require the city to initiate eminent domain proceedings to acquire the electric facilities of PG&E within its jurisdiction. It would also set a precedent that would likely have an impact on other jurisdictions in the state, enticing them to go into the electric business as well. A defeat of the measure would bid well for PG&E in its quest to stave off such actions.

My boss had seen all this coming. The three-day trip that our team had taken to the northern region was intended to rehearse the "dog and pony" show for Berkeley, and I was on the team specifically for the Battle of Berkeley.

As the campaign began to heat up during the latter part of February, Dick was the chief PG&E spokesman and lead debater on the "takeover" issue. He began to include me in all of his debates, insisting that I become more actively involved in making presentations. I quickly found out that, regardless of my initial hesitation about the assignment, I was no longer an alien in a strange land. Dick showcased me more and more in debates, and, most importantly, he assigned me to make a number of media appearances that he would normally have made himself.

I could not help thinking, *Perhaps the appearance of a young Black lawyer debating on behalf of PG&E may not be a bad idea in liberal Berkeley.*

That was a career boost for me. To be sure, I was lucky, because, in addition to having confidence in me, Dick had an ulterior motive. Thus, he pushed me into the forefront to become the face of the company in a very liberal city that would probably be more accepting of me as spokesman for PG&E than it would be of him.

I did my job, and Dick's wisdom paid off. The election was very close, with PG&E winning 52 percent of the vote to remain the electric provider. The company was jubilant, as was I. They had used me, but I had also used them. It was a double win!

And so, from the beginning of my career at PG&E, I learned to exploit opportunities to distinguish myself. But I also learned that the key is to position yourself as a valuable asset without appearing to be self-serving. I was afforded another opportunity to do that within my first six months on the job.

In March 1973, I was contacted by Eugene Scoles, the Dean of the University of Oregon Law School in Eugene. After identifying himself, he indicated that Dean Ed Halbach of my alma mater, Boalt Hall, had suggested that I would be an excellent candidate for the Oregon law school faculty.

That was a big surprise to me, since I had no real relationship with Dean Halbach and was unaware of any interest he had in my future. Obviously, I was greatly appreciative that Dean Halbach had recommended me for consideration.

What an honor to be sought after for a law school faculty! But as a new lawyer at PG&E, how could I consider leaving so soon?

Fortunately, my next thought was that this might not only be a career alternative, but also a chance to subtly let PG&E know that others were interested in my talents. With that second thought, I decided to see where this opportunity would lead.

Following that interesting phone conversation, Dean Scoles invited me to come to Oregon to meet with the law school faculty. At that point, I knew he was serious. He indicated that there was no guarantee how the faculty would view me, but I would have every opportunity to impress them, and the outcome would depend on that. But he was certain that I would be well received, since I had come highly recommended by Dean Halbach.

I said that I would have to discuss the opportunity with my wife, because moving to Oregon would entail uprooting our young children, Tony and Regina, who were 9 and 7 at the time. After I discussed the matter with Esther, we decided that it made sense to at least explore this possibility.

I thought, *Why not let PG&E know that I have other options, especially since I fought so hard to get on its legal staff in the first place?*

I considered this a good opportunity to impress upon PG&E that the academic world was interested in my skills, so they were lucky to have me. Nevertheless, I would never have stated that to them. If I were made an offer, they would find out and reach their own conclusions.

So, at the expense of the law school, Esther and I flew up to Oregon on a rainy evening in March. The rain was no surprise, since it frequently rains in Oregon, which was one of the negative factors in our decision-making. Scheduled to remain in Eugene for two days, we were met at the airport by someone from the law school, who took us to a hotel downtown. That was the first time either of us had been to the city. The next day, I was scheduled to make a presentation to the faculty on a legal subject of my choice. The purpose of this, of course, was for the faculty to assess my ability to analyze and speak to complex legal issues. After that, the faculty would question me to determine if I could defend my position in a scholarly manner. I had sent the materials to the faculty in advance for their review and preparation.

The United States Supreme Court had recently issued a ruling in the Otter Tail Power Company case, which dealt with whether antitrust laws applied to public utilities. This was my area and the case was novel, so I had chosen it as the focus of my presentation.

I arrived at the school two hours early to get a feel for the campus, which was beautiful and certainly a place conducive to academic learning. At the meeting, everyone was most gracious, and I could not have been in a friendlier environment. Finally, the time came for my presentation.

I had just turned 29, and felt very assured of myself, although I was somewhat anxious to make a good presentation to a distinguished faculty. As I suspected, all the professors were White males, mostly over 40. But, just as I had recited the titles of the books of the Bible to a large congregation when I was a little boy, I spoke with confidence and then took questions in a spirited exchange, which went very well.

That evening, Esther and I attended a reception sponsored by the university so that we could meet other members of the faculty outside of the law school. That's when we discovered that there were two Black faculty members in the entire university, both of whom were there. That certainly was a drawback.

My acceptance of an invitation to apply for the faculty position could not be kept a secret from PG&E, because part of the application process required the law school to contact my current employer for a performance assessment, which they did.

Responding to this request on May 9, 1973, the PG&E general counsel who headed the legal department, Fred Searles, wrote the following. "One of the significant measures of Mr. Harris's worth is that I would be quite unhappy to lose him from our staff and do not relish lending aid to such a possibility. I must say, however, that he has shown all-round capabilities...and could be expected to do a good job in any field of legal work, including the academic field."

As I had hoped, Dean Scoles extended an invitation for me to join the faculty. In our telephone conversation, I expressed my deep appreciation for the offer, but declined. He expressed his disappointment and made it clear that the offer would stand for the future as well, should I change my mind. That was, indeed, great news, just in case something went south at PG&E, and I needed a backup plan. Word spread rapidly throughout the legal department, as I suspected it would. I was very pleased. To be offered to teach at a major law school was a big plus in the eyes of my colleagues.

I spent little time thinking about how grateful I was to be at PG&E, instead focusing on how to thrive there. I was eager to assess every opportunity to distinguish myself, and so, for example, when I received an unexpected offer from the California State Bar to be a bar exam grader, I readily accepted, knowing that only a few select lawyers ever get that chance. At PG&E, it was considered an asset.

However, what I found to be most critical to my success in the legal department during my early years was preparation, preparation, and more preparation. I had been raised to believe—as most Black youngsters were when I was growing up—that you have to be "twice as good as the White man" to be competitive. So, my strategy was simply to work longer and harder than most of my colleagues. Often I was the first person in the office, arriving as early as 6:00, and I frequently put in twelve or more hours. The key to my success was time management, and, fortunately for me, I only needed six hours of sleep a night. Also, working for Dick Clarke served to reinforce my work ethic. Dick argued that if you seek perfection, you'll be one of the best, so I put in the time necessary to live up to his expectations.

15

Trial in Redding

Question everything. Every stripe, every star, every word spoken. Everything.

—Ernest Gaines

In April 1973, after PG&E defeated the attempted takeover in Berkeley, I sat with Dick Clarke to explain to him that while I enjoyed working with him, and was practicing exactly the kind of law I wanted to practice, I needed to understand the court system and wanted to enhance my experience with trial work.

Although Dick understood my wishes, he was quite clear about one thing: for him, the legal department was a stepping stone for mobility into the business side of the company, and he wanted me to know that it should be the same for me. While teaching me to be a good lawyer, he also motivated me to take every opportunity to learn the operations of the company. Assuring me that I would eventually get bored by litigating cases, he did, however, arrange for me to get the experience.

The litigation section of the legal department was headed by an assistant general counsel named Charlie Van Duesen, who was distinguishable by the bow ties he always wore. I would work on what Dick called "fender benders." A PG&E service truck would get into an accident, and the company would have to defend the case. Dick told me that I didn't want to become a trial lawyer, spending all my time on fender benders, but he understood my desire to get a feel for the court system. Thus, my caseload was divided between working for Dick on high-profile corporate matters and dealing with my litigation cases. The cases acquainted me with the court: how to file a complaint; how to answer a complaint; how to file a motion; how to take a deposition; and how to appear before a judge.

One of my assignments was a wrongful death case. In discussing it with me, Charlie said it had been pending for several years, and there was no question that PG&E was liable. It was only a matter of how much money we would be liable for when we went to court. Charlie saw little risk in my handling the case, since we could not win it anyway. It was a clear loser, and therefore, as he saw it, the case would be good for me to learn from. I was to proceed with depositions and other matters to move the case to trial and get it resolved without the company having to pay huge damages. Since it was a wrongful death case, I knew it would have a lot more learning potential for me than the fender benders did, so I was pleased with the opportunity.

The facts of the case were horrible. A seven-year-old girl had been killed in a fire in Uno, California, which is right outside Redding. According to the complaint, PG&E's electric transformer had failed to operate correctly, and consequently allowed an electric surge to penetrate the house, igniting a fire that destroyed the home, killed the girl, and injured other family members. The case was a real tragedy, with lots of sympathy for the mother of the young victim. It was unlikely that there would be any mercy for PG&E. As Charlie told me, "It's just a matter of how much PG&E is going to have to pay."

When I received the case, it was already five years old. I reviewed volumes of material and began to think there was possibly an opportunity to win. The expectations were so low, why not try? When I discussed this with a lawyer who had previously been assigned the case, he thought that I was hilariously optimistic to think the case could be won. Without telling Charlie that I wanted to prove that I could win the case, I quietly continued to schedule depositions and retain expert witnesses, so I could learn as much as possible about the case and what I thought I would need to win it.

Charlie was curious about why I was spending so much time on a case that had no chance of avoiding liability. I assured him that I was doing it to get experience in how to try a case that we believed we would lose. He understood my point and allowed me to go on with elaborate preparations to defend a "loser." In my book, Charlie was cool, and I liked him very much for that.

As is customary, whenever PG&E tried a case outside the Bay Area, local counsel was retained to work with the PG&E lawyer. In Redding, our retained local counsel was an older gentleman named Larry Kennedy, who was affable and a pleasure to get to know. A former Regent of the University of California, Larry was well known and well respected in the Redding area. Before the trial, I made several visits to Redding, although Larry never really participated with me in the preparations. Like Charlie, he had concluded that we had no chance of winning, but this was a good opportunity for me to get some litigation experience. Yet, he was always available to answer any questions I had.

A few weeks before the trial, a strange and unexpected thing happened, which threw me for a loop: the opposing counsel waived trial by jury, allowing the case to be tried by the judge. I was stunned, for that made no sense to me. I could not figure out why the opposing counsel wanted a trial by court rather than by jury in a friendly jurisdiction. But that meant I would no longer have to face a jury, which most likely would be anxious to extract revenge from PG&E for the child's death.

That was my first big break, but I still knew the case was a long shot at best. The trial was set for the last week of March 1974 in the Shasta County Superior Court in Redding, a relatively small, almost entirely White city, northeast of San Francisco. The case would be tried by conservative Superior Court Judge Richard B. Eaton, who, like Charlie, always wore bow ties. I wondered if there were any connection, but obviously there was not.

By now, I had been a member of the bar for approximately fifteen months, and here I was, on the eve of trying my first major case.

Where else could I get this kind of legal experience, except at PG&E?

For the first time, I felt really good about having been rejected by every major law firm in San Francisco, because if I had been hired by one of them, only in my dreams would I have found myself in the position of trying a major case with *no* courtroom experience. I had invested an enormous amount of time and energy on the case, and had clearly done far more than was reasonable to prepare it, because I secretly wanted to show my superiors that a Black lawyer could not only meet expectations, but do the "impossible."

The trial began with the plaintiffs presenting the tearful testimony of the dead girl's mother. She said that on February 25, 1969, around 2:00 A.M., she awoke feeling heat from a fire, although she didn't see any flames. Her testimony was extremely emotional, detailing how she was able to save two of her children from the fire, but was unable to save the third. As she described the events of the fire, she broke down in tears several times. Had there been a jury hearing the case, it's likely that one or more members would have broken down, too. Because of the mother's fragile emotional state, I elected not to cross-examine her. Perhaps too much Perry Mason, but I thought I would only bring out more tears and elicit sympathy from the judge, which I did not want.

The mother's boyfriend, who was living with her in the house at the time of the fire, was next on the stand. He testified that the house was constantly blowing fuses, and that a stereo had been repaired before the fire, due to electrical damage. Because of my extensive preparation, I had figured out the plaintiffs' strategy. To prove liability, they intended to present an expert witness, who would testify that the electric transformer was faulty, allowing too much power to enter the house, thereby causing the electrical problems the boyfriend described, and ultimately causing a spark that ignited the fire.

I had retained my own experts to review the possible causes of the blaze. One key piece of evidence was the PG&E meter attached to the house, which had nothing wrong with it.

Had the fire been electrical in origin, the meter should have detected a surge.

My theory was that the fire had been started by a wood stove that was overstoked before the family went to bed. They were trying to keep the home heated for a longer time by cramming the stove, which made the pipe get really hot. Since it was routed through the attic of the home, I reasoned that some debris in the attic had come in touch with the hot pipe, thereby igniting a fire. Having grown up in rural Arkansas, in a house without central heating, I was familiar with similar wood stoves. I could still hear my Daddy saying, "Don't put too much wood in, boy, or you'll burn this house down!"

So, I was prepared to aggressively attack the plaintiffs' theory of the electric transformer being the cause of the fire. My chief expert was a Dr. Lewis, a professor of electrical engineering in Missouri, who had written several books on electricity and educated me on the subject. Another expert was a retired PG&E consultant, Ira Collins, who had years of experience with electric transformers and meters.

The plaintiffs' chief expert was John Maddox, a Fire Science instructor at Shasta College. When I had deposed Maddox, I recognized that he was very knowledgeable about Fire Science, but did not seem to know much about electricity. The night before Maddox testified, I spent considerable time with Larry Kennedy, talking about how I should attack Maddox on cross-examination. When I explained to Larry that I thought I could get Maddox disqualified from testifying on electrical matters, Larry thought I was joking.

"Bob," he said, "there's no way Judge Eaton is going to disqualify this fire expert from testifying that the transformer caused the fire. It's wishful thinking."

"Don't you think I should give it a try?"

"Of course, you should try," he responded, "but the judge is going to allow him to testify on the issue."

After Maddox was sworn in, I immediately objected to his testifying as an expert on electricity, which startled the opposing counsel. After I explained the basis of my objection, the judge allowed me to question Maddox about his expertise. My strategy was not to prevent him from testifying about the fire, but rather about the cause of the fire, which was at the heart of the plaintiffs' theory concerning PG&E's liability. Failure to prove that the fire had been ignited by an electrical source would absolve PG&E of liability.

I could see the look of worry on the opposing counsel's face as I proceeded to ask Maddox about his educational background and his experience, especially regarding electricity. As I grilled him, I suspected that he would be unable to answer most of my questions, which proved to be correct. He was growing increasingly frustrated with my electricity questions, which went on for twenty minutes, before I decided that it was time to go for the jugular.

"Mister Maddox," I said, "can you explain to the court the difference between a 'C' transformer and an 'S' transformer?"

He paused for a long time, before admitting that he could not.

"Your Honor," I said, turning to the judge, "I move that Mister Maddox be disqualified from testifying as an expert on the issue of electricity being the cause of the fire."

Without hesitation, Judge Eaton responded, "Motion granted. Mister Maddox, you will not be allowed to address the issue of electricity as a cause of the fire."

I was shocked, as was the opposing counsel. Larry, on the other hand, smiled and gave me a look that said, "Well, I guess I was wrong."

During recess, which was shortly after the judge's ruling, I noticed a Black gentleman in his sixties, sitting in the back of the courtroom. He had apparently slipped in during the Maddox testimony. It was strange to see him, because during the entire week I had spent in Redding, I had not seen a single Black face. As I passed by, he jumped from his seat and came rushing up to me.

"Brother," he said, "I don't know who you are, or what you were talking about up there, but you sure were telling them White folks off. I'm proud of you."

That touched my heart and kindled my resolve. It was a moment of solidarity between two Black men.

It is really hard to explain what it feels like to be a Black man in America. Nobel Prize–winning author Toni Morrison once wrote: "Definitions belong to the definers, not the defined." I know who I am, including my strengths and my weaknesses, but in America I am constantly smacked by racist assumptions that I am not fully human. That notion was used as a justification for slavery. It is a deeply held belief, despite all the evidence to the contrary, that still persists to this day. So, when that Black gentleman said, "I'm proud of you," I understood exactly what he was trying to communicate. In response, I told him who I was and what the case was about. I appreciated the support. He left the courtroom, never to be seen by me again.

Since the plaintiffs had no other "electrical expert," the rest of the case went fairly routinely, including the testimony of Dr. Lewis and the PG&E meter expert, both of whom said that the fire could not have been ignited by an electrical source. My final witness was a fire prevention expert from the Redding area, who testified that the most likely cause of the fire was an overstoked wood stove.

Judge Eaton delivered his verdict the day after closing arguments. While I was not sure how he would rule, I was greatly relieved when he took the bench and said that he was rendering a verdict in favor of PG&E. When I called Charlie, back in the San Francisco office, he could not believe we had won.

"Are you *sure* we won?" he asked.

We had won. That victory sent shock waves through PG&E's legal department. The lesson I took away was this: When others say that something cannot be done, continue to cling to your intuition. But you also need to be soundly prepared. You cannot allow yourself to be thwarted by those little voices, including your own, that imply, "You're just an inexperienced token here; you're not as good as the rest of them."

On the other hand, you cannot be overconfident. One of my outside mentors, Tom Berkley, had warned me, "You can't rest on your laurels, ever. You will always be held to a different standard." Whatever the assignment, he said, "Don't complain, just do it."

The subtle intimidation of always having to prove yourself can be debilitating, even paralyzing, for some young Black professionals who are trying to climb the corporate ladder in overwhelmingly White settings. That's one reason it helps to have trusted wise mentors, and it is also a reason to make valuable connections wherever you can.

From my very first day in the PG&E legal department, my goal was to meet everyone and to make the effort to bridge the racial and experiential gaps between my colleagues and me. I could have waited for them to make me feel comfortable, but I considered it my responsibility to make *them* feel comfortable with *me*. I decided to go into each lawyer's office, introduce myself, and ask each one about his experiences with the company and his areas of interest in the law. They would share what they were working on and were very happy to talk about their past successes. I listened and I learned. Listening was far more important to me than attempting to impress them with what I knew.

Almost every day, I went to lunch with one or more of my colleagues. After work, I would sometimes join other lawyers for drinks. I did that frequently enough to be sociable, but not regularly. I had a wife and young children, as well as other responsibilities, so I joined my colleagues as often as I could, in order not to give the impression that I was an outsider. Whether or not you fit in is your responsibility. Others cannot bring you into the group. You must introduce yourself. Others may choose to exclude you, but that will be more likely to happen if you have done something to alienate yourself from them.

At PG&E, there was no shortage of opportunities to fraternize. The legal department was part of a softball league with other in-house corporate law departments and Bay Area law firms. Win or lose, we met for pizza and beer after the games. We also had an annual Christmas party, which gave us a chance to be introduced to wives and significant others. Soon enough, senior attorneys began inviting Esther and me to their homes.

In addition to establishing myself in the legal department, I made it a point to meet other Black professionals at PG&E. In 1972, when I started, there were five of us: Owen Davis, Ed Phillips, Roosevelt Mosley, Bunnie Brown, and me—all of us tokens in our respective departments.

Owen was a distinguished engineer with a nuclear background. In 1985, he rose to become the company's first Black officer. His service in upper management was brief, however, for his life was tragically cut short in 1987 by pancreatic cancer.

Ed Phillips and Roosevelt Mosley were relatively young engineers, who had been recruited from historically Black colleges. Roosevelt only spent three years at PG&E before returning to Mississippi to work near his family, but Ed spent the rest of his career with the company.

It was Bunnie Brown, who had a sharp, inquisitive mind and a sense of urgency, who really shook things up racially at PG&E. She had started in Customer Service, but quickly worked her way up in the corporate headquarters to Personnel, as the Human Resources Department was called at the time. Bunnie had access to raw employment data, and it was clear to me that she was on a mission.

The operating units that actually provided gas and electric services were fairly well integrated at the time; and among union employees, Blacks were well represented in most divisions at lower levels. But in the corporate cafeteria, there were only the five of us, who would meet regularly for lunch, chatting informally, learning from each other's experiences, and offering support to each other.

But Bunnie had a specific goal. She felt strongly that Blacks should permeate the company beyond operations, needing to become part of management. One of us, she said, had to break through the upper management doors with an appointment to officer level.

We all agreed. I think we had a collective sense that this was our responsibility. Others before us had made our success possible, so we had a duty to pave the way for those who would follow.

Bunnie had the ear of John Cooper, the vice president of personnel, to whom she took her ideas and the essential goals of our discussions. Although she was passionate, she wasn't shoving her cause down anyone's throat. With her savoir-faire and natural charm, she figured out a way to set up regular meetings between our group and Cooper.

The first personnel meeting in the vice president's office made quite an impression on me, since I had never been in the office of a senior executive before, other than the general counsel's office in the legal department. The office of the vice president of personnel was huge by comparison and elegantly appointed. It even had a fireplace, something I had never seen in an office before.

Our group, which was reduced to four after Roosevelt Mosley returned to the South, met intermittently in that office for about a year before the company took action. The first concrete result of our meetings was the promotion of Owen Davis as the San Francisco Division Manager. Over time, our group unlocked the doors for many Black professionals who came through PG&E. We laid the foundation for the founding of the company's Black Employees Association. Without question, our mutual support made it possible for me to survive and thrive at the company.

16

Networking

The function of freedom is to free someone else.

—Toni Morrison

In my early days at PG&E, aside from learning how to become a good attorney, I focused on networking with other Black professionals, both inside and outside the company. The first important contact I made was with Tom Berkley. One day I noticed him walking down the hall in the legal department. As he passed the open door of my office, he glanced in, stopped dead in his tracks, turned around, and introduced himself. At the time, Tom was one of the most noted Black attorneys in the Bay Area, as well as a successful businessman, the owner of a Black newspaper in the East Bay, *The Oakland Post*, among other enterprises. In Northern California, he was a legend.

Tom was a very engaging man, over six feet tall, with a broad smile and huge piercing eyes. When he sat down in my office that day, he let me know that he was there to see Dick Clarke, with whom he had a long professional relationship. His intention, he said, was to persuade PG&E to place more ads in his newspaper, since he felt that the Black press was not getting its fair share of advertising dollars. He also wanted some of the outside legal work that the company contracted lawyers in private practice to do.

Most of our conversation, however, was not about his goals. Instead, for the half-hour that we talked, Tom essentially interviewed me. Afterward, he made it clear that he was pleased to see that PG&E had hired me, a young Black attorney, and he offered to make himself available to assist me in the future. That was the beginning of a twenty-five-year friendship, which lasted until his death in 2001.

Every three or four months, Tom and I had lunch together at various restaurants throughout the Bay Area. In addition, he often invited me to his newspaper office, where we would spend considerable time discussing issues, most of them about civil rights. I was motivated by Tom's success in facing power and demanding a piece of the pie. He taught me a great deal about how to get ahead.

During my first few years at PG&E, I thought seriously about where I wanted to go in my legal career and how to best use my legal expertise in and for the Black community. Although I loved what I was doing for the company, I did miss the sense of satisfaction that I had felt on almost a daily basis when I worked as a probation officer, trying to help Black youth to get on the right track.

More than anything else, I wanted to follow in the footsteps of one of my heroes, Charles Hamilton Houston, a giant among Black attorneys. A graduate of Harvard Law School, Houston made a name for himself in civil rights as Dean of the Howard University Law School and as the first legal defense counsel for the NAACP.

"A lawyer," he once said, "is either a social engineer or a parasite on society." I knew I didn't want to be the latter.

Immediately after my admission to the California Bar, I became a member of the Charles Houston Law Club, the only organization of Black lawyers in the Bay Area, which had been founded in 1955. I attended my first meeting in January 1973, at the Oakland home of Hiawatha T. Roberts, who three years later would second my nomination as vice president of the National Bar Association. Founded in Iowa in 1925, the NBA is an organization of Black attorneys that was created at a time when the American Bar Association refused to admit Black lawyers.

At that meeting in 1973, I saw more Black lawyers gathered together—twenty to twenty-five of us—than I had seen before in my whole life. The purpose of the meeting was to plan for the 1973 annual convention of the NBA that summer at the newly constructed Hyatt Regency Hotel at the Embarcadero Center in San Francisco. Among other things, we discussed how to raise money for the event, recommended speakers and seminars, and scheduled professional and social activities.

Everyone was thrilled about hosting the first NBA convention in Northern California. Since the organization's power structure was controlled exclusively outside the West Coast, this was a chance for the Bay Area to show off. That first meeting of mine set in motion events which charted a course that, two years later, led to my election as assistant secretary of the NBA. A year after that, I was elected as the first vice president of the organization to come from the West Coast. To this day, no other individual in NBA history has ever been elected to a high position within such a short time out of law school. My ascension began when I met a dynamic attorney at that meeting who would take me under his wing and push me into prominence in the association.

His name was Benjamin Travis, a charismatic leader who was chairman of the local host Resources Committee for the upcoming convention, which put him in charge of fundraising.

When I introduced myself as a new lawyer at PG&E, Ben immediately said, "This little brother is going to be on my committee."

With Judge Travis (left) and Tom Berkley

He made it clear to me that, because I worked for PG&E, he expected me to assist him in obtaining corporate resources for the convention, something his committee had not yet been able to accomplish because of a lack of access to corporate contributors. I told him that I would do what I could.

"Little brother," he said, "I know you can make it happen." (He called all the younger male lawyers "Little Brother.")

Soon after that, I was able to arrange for Ben to meet with Rick Todd, PG&E's Manager of Governmental Affairs. When Ben and I arrived at the meeting in Rick's office on the thirtieth floor of the company's corporate headquarters, Ben was sporting a huge Afro and full beard. He looked somewhat like Frederick Douglass, which I am sure startled Rick and everyone else who saw him. Nevertheless, Ben articulated cogent arguments for why PG&E should support the NBA convention and convince other corporations to do the same.

Obviously intrigued by Ben, Rick assured him of PG&E's support and named a number of other major corporations in San Francisco that he would contact for contributions. True to his word, within a few weeks Rick had secured an unbelievable sum of money for that time—more than $40,000—from PG&E and the other contributors. In the end, we actually had money left over that we were unable to spend!

During that summer convention, it became clear that the Charles Houston Law Club needed to become a more viable association of Black lawyers in Northern California. The task of building the club's clout and membership fell to Ben. When he was elected president in early 1974, he recommended the officers who would serve with him. John Stewart became vice president, Hiram Smith became treasurer, and I became secretary.

"Little brother," Ben said, "I want you because you can produce. Being secretary is an important position, since you will be the chief communicator between leadership and membership."

The position gave me instant visibility at a time when I was less than two years out of law school.

Our leadership team laid out our top priorities, chief of which was to build the membership of the Charles Houston Law Club to at least eighty percent of the Black lawyers in Northern California. To be effective, we had to show that we had strength in numbers. To increase our membership, we first had to identify with names and addresses all the Black lawyers out there, of whom there were approximately one hundred at the time. When we made contact, we had to offer them reasons why they needed to join the club.

To do that, we became involved with a number of community endeavors and took on a number of controversial issues to demonstrate our relevance. We established a newsletter and persuaded Dale Rubin, my old friend at Boalt Hall, to be its editor. Dale's editorial comments were a lightning rod for controversy. There was no issue that he didn't have an opinion on, and his comments were specifically designed to get lawyers riled up. He succeeded.

By 1975, we had been so effective in executing our strategy that we had as members almost ninety percent of the Black lawyers in the Bay Area. When we had identified them, some of our effort led to unexpected outcomes. For example, one lawyer we identified as Black, who worked at a big law firm, made it clear to us that he did not want to be identified with Black attorneys. We were puzzled because, given his chocolate skin color, he could not have been passing for White. We apologized to him, but within a few months, he was no longer at the firm. After that, we couldn't help wondering if his refusal to join our organization might have changed the course of his career.

The association grew under Ben's leadership, and I grew

under Ben's visionary strategies. He had ideas and suggestions, and believed in executing them. Motivating others to work with him was one of his greatest talents, and I was gladly his right-hand man. Whenever he gave me an assignment, it always was accompanied by the same words of encouragement: "Little brother, you can figure out how to make it happen." That helped me to develop as a strategist. Ben was always in the forefront in providing a vision and dreams of what might be. His tenure as president of the club only lasted a little over a year, because he was appointed by Governor Jerry Brown to the Oakland Municipal Court in early 1975.

At the time, I felt as if I were living in two different worlds—PG&E and the Charles Houston Law Club—not to mention my fraternity. Fortunately, my boss at PG&E, Dick Clarke, was supportive of my outside activities. If he had not been, it's likely that my career at PG&E would have been short-lived. Dick readily saw my community involvement as beneficial to the company. After all, he had seen firsthand the impact of my involvement with the takeover election in Berkeley. Public relations guru that he was, Dick firmly believed that corporations should be connected to the communities they serve. Frankly, I did not leave that connection to chance or a change of heart. I would occasionally ask the bar and others to communicate with PG&E, thanking it for its support. That always went over well.

17

Stay the Course

*A battle is won by the side that is absolutely
determined to win.*

—Leo Tolstoy

After Ben left to take up his judgeship, I was elected
president to succeed him. With a healthy enrollment, we
applied to the California State Bar Association to be designated
as an official affiliate, which would make us more effective in
the legal arena by putting us in a better position to argue on
behalf of Black lawyers.

Our opportunity to act as a bar association occurred
almost immediately when we encountered bias in Alameda
County's policy on retaining lawyers for criminal defendants.
In situations where those defendants could not afford the
costs of legal representation, the court appointed and paid for
lawyers in private practice to represent them. That work could
be lucrative, and sometimes the cases were significant enough
to attract publicity, which gave the lawyers free advertising. At
the time, the Alameda County courts were contracting with the
Alameda County Bar Association, which was then responsible

for referring criminal cases to private lawyers when the Public Defender had a conflict. However, criminal defense work was not distributed fairly. The more lucrative criminal defense cases and the more serious crimes were routinely referred to White lawyers. The rationale for this, given by the Alameda County Bar Association, was that Black lawyers did not meet the requirement for years of experience. That system of referring cases on the basis of seniority clearly disfavored Black attorneys, which we deemed unfair.

Initially, representatives of the Charles Houston Bar Association (CHBA), as we were now known, attempted to sit down with members of the Alameda County Bar Association to persuade them to adjust the distribution of cases. When these meetings proved fruitless, the CHBA filed a racial discrimination lawsuit against the Alameda County Bar Association and the County of Alameda.

Because of my legal experience in the area of constitutional law, the CHBA appointed me to be the lead attorney. In court, I was aided by Hiawatha T. Roberts, a brilliant lawyer and one of the thirty-two founding members of the club, and by Professor Henry Ramsey, who had taught me criminal law at Boalt Hall, and was the only Black member of the faculty when I graduated. Ramsey had also been a Deputy District Attorney in neighboring Contra Costa County and had spent several years in private practice before becoming a councilman in Berkeley and an academic. Clearly, he was brilliant by all standards.

We argued that the Alameda County Bar Association's system of referring criminal cases to private lawyers was discriminatory. However, the judge ruled against us.

Truthfully, that is what we had expected. Our strategy was to get as much publicity as possible, letting the community know how their tax dollars were being spent, with the goal of shaming the Alameda County Bar Association enough to get it to reconsider its policy. After we lost the case, we sat down at the negotiating table once again. This time, however, we persuaded the county and the County Bar Association to develop a new referral system. It was still unbalanced, but it was fairer than before. We had lost the court battle, but we had won the real fight of getting more opportunities for Black lawyers. Thereafter, CHBA was perceived as a fighter who was unwilling to be pushed over.

A few months later, the CHBA took on an even larger issue: police brutality. The NAACP had been loudly complaining for years about systemic police brutality against Black people in the Bay Area. Whenever the NAACP held a press conference or issued a press release criticizing the police for brutality, various police officers' associations, including those in San Francisco and Oakland, filed defamation lawsuits. The police argued that the written and verbal complaints defamed the police officers in question. The defamation cases were a new strategy being applied by police officers' associations across the nation to intimidate the NAACP into silence, by putting it in a position in which it could not afford to defend itself.

However, the NAACP had a wealth of legal talent, both Black and White, who were willing to work pro bono on its behalf, including the CHBA. For the Bay Area case, I was the lead attorney on a team that was supervised by Nathaniel S. Colley, Sr., a longtime civil rights lawyer out of Sacramento, and we also had the advice of the general counsel from the national office of the NAACP. Others on the CHBA team included George Holland, Tom Broome, and John Burris.

The San Francisco and Oakland police associations stepped up their intimidation tactics by amending their complaint to specifically sue two young Black attorneys who worked for the NAACP, as well as the organization itself. Those lawyers had castigated the police in various press conferences, so we expanded our defense work to protect them.

In the end, we successfully defended both the NAACP and the attorneys against those baseless lawsuits. Our winning argument was that the NAACP had a First Amendment right to complain about police brutality, and that the police officers' associations could not invoke defamation to silence their critics. Both the San Francisco County Superior Court and the Alameda County Superior Court agreed with us, granting summary judgments in the cases. When the decisions were appealed, the California Court of Appeals sustained the lower court rulings in our favor.

Receiving the NAACP's Highest Legal Honor,
the William Robert Ming Award

In 1986, I would be given the NAACP's William Robert Ming Award for legal advocacy, its highest legal honor, for my work on those cases.

In addition to my outside work assisting in organizing the Black legal community in Northern California and directing its pro bono services on behalf of the Black community—a huge endeavor by any measure—I was also being urged to assume greater leadership in my fraternity, Kappa Alpha Psi. When I say I was "being urged," that's not to say that I needed to be pushed. At that time, 1973, I was a very ambitious young man. Although I had just gotten my feet wet by serving as Polemarch (president) of the Berkeley Alumni Chapter, when I was encouraged to move up, I was ready—or at least I thought I was.

The Berkeley Alumni Chapter was one of dozens in the Western Province of the fraternity, a territory that at that time included Alaska, Arizona, California, Hawaii, Idaho, Nevada, Oregon, and Washington. The highest position in a Province was, and still is, Province Polemarch. The number 2 position was Senior Province Vice Polemarch—and that was the position my supporters encouraged me to seek.

In 1973, the Western Province convention was held in San Jose, my backyard, so I arrived there fully confident that I had considerable support. However, the Southern California members had their own candidate, a member of the Los Angeles Alumni Chapter who was a graduate student earning a doctoral degree in psychology. I was a working lawyer, and my opponent was still in school! Surely, the delegates would conclude that I was better suited to assume a leadership role when our credentials were presented ahead of the vote. Wrong!

What I learned is that votes are best secured long before an election. The outcome in my case was that I lost when I had fully expected to win. I had obviously underestimated my opponent, who had campaigned in ways that I had not. He knew the number of delegate votes he needed to garner from the various chapters throughout the Province to win the election. He also had the advantage that there were more chapters in Southern California than in Northern California. In my blinding arrogance, I had not seriously calculated that. When I went into the convention, I didn't even know the number of votes that I was sure to get—or, worse yet, the number of votes I needed to win.

While others in my camp were shocked and upset, I learned a valuable lesson from that defeat. In the future, I would be better prepared for elections, taking nothing for granted. In fact, I never lost another election in any organization. Moreover, in 1991, at our Grand Chapter meeting in Orlando, Florida, I was elected the twenty-seventh Grand Polemarch of Kappa Alpha Psi.

After my defeat in San Jose, I continued to serve as Polemarch of the Berkeley Alumni Chapter, and through that position I made contributions to the entire Western Province, making sure that others took note of that. I was consciously and deliberately planting seeds for future support. The graduate student who had defeated me in San Jose and who had been serving as Senior Province Vice Polemarch turned out to be unimpressive. So, at our next annual meeting, when he was up for reelection, I beat him!

Within a few months, when the head of the Western Province, the Province Polemarch, announced that he was stepping down, I was ready for another campaign. According to our fraternity rules at that time, the Grand Polemarch appointed the Polemarchs of all the various Provinces, but his decision was based on recommendations from the members of the Provinces. Therefore, at our next annual Western Province Council meeting, in San Diego, a vote would be taken to recommend candidates to the Grand Polemarch.

With the urging of many brothers, I announced my candidacy for the position and began campaigning well in advance of the convention. When I arrived in San Diego, I had already secured many votes and went after more. I took the time to speak personally with as many voting delegates as I could, sharing my credentials as well as my vision for the Province. Those personal contacts made a considerable difference.

In San Diego, my chapter nominated me for Province Polemarch, and I received all but four of the votes. A done deal? No.

18

The Politics of Leadership

*If you have no confidence in self, you are twice
defeated in the race of life. With confidence, you
have won even before you have started.*

—Marcus Garvey

I now faced a new obstacle: despite the overwhelming
vote in my favor, the Grand Polemarch, Dr. E. E. Allen, who
was at the San Diego meeting, genuinely believed that I was
not ready, because I was one of the youngest brothers that the
Province had ever presented to be Province Polemarch. Dr.
Allen, a fiftyish dentist from Shreveport, Louisiana, did not
have confidence that the older brothers in the Province would
follow the leadership of a 31-year-old upstart. He was also
doubtful, because of my youth, that I would fit in well with
the national leadership. Typically, the youngest Province
Polemarch was in his forties.

I had a spirited private discussion with Brother Allen in his
hotel room about his assessment, in the course of which I tried
to explain why I fervently believed that I would prove to be

highly effective. After a while, however, it became clear that I was not making any progress, so I returned to my room to meet with my group of fervent supporters: Charles "Jack" Sudduth, who was a former Province Polemarch; James L. Bradford, who was the Province Keeper of the Records; and James O. Whaley, who was the current Province Polemarch—all of them my elders and mentors. After listening to me recount my unsuccessful meeting with the Grand Polemarch, all three told me essentially to "cool it" and let *them* take care of it.

My three mentors, with Jack Sudduth in the lead, pulled the Grand Polemarch aside and had a "come to Jesus" meeting with him. After that exchange, Dr. Allen invited me to speak with him again, but this time his attitude toward me had changed. He let me know that my three supporters had convinced him that he would be making a huge mistake if he failed to choose me. Thus, he issued an announcement to the entire fraternity that I had been appointed the fifteenth Polemarch of the Western Province.

Not long after my appointment, I had to fly to Philadelphia to attend a summit of the Province Polemarchs. All twelve of us came from different parts of the nation to gather for a weekend meeting at the Hilton Hotel. After an uneventful flight from San Francisco, I arrived at the Philadelphia airport around 5:00 P.M. on a Thursday evening, took a cab to the hotel, walked in, and presented my reservation slip to a White woman at the front desk. She told me that there were no more rooms available. My secretary at PG&E had confirmed my reservation and had let the hotel know that I would probably be checking in by evening, so I asked the clerk to check again.

"Nothing's available at this time," she said without

blinking.

Since she said that the room was not available "at this time," I assumed it would come available shortly, so I sat down in a chair across the lobby. While I was waiting, I looked again at my reservation slip, and confirmed that it was accurate.

In a few minutes, another Province Polemarch approached the front desk. He had not yet seen me as he presented his reservation slip and then shook his head while the front desk clerk spoke to him. When he saw me, he came over, and we talked about our confirmed reservations, our inability to get a room at the hotel, and our shock at finding that the reservations were not being honored. As we talked, several White men walked up to the front desk with their suitcases and were immediately given keys to their rooms. What was going on? Knowing that something was wrong, we returned to the front desk to try again.

"No rooms are available," the woman said.

This was 1975, eleven years after the Civil Rights Act of 1964, which had outlawed discrimination in public accommodations. Furthermore, this wasn't the South, where some vestiges of segregation still existed. We were in the birthplace of the nation on the eve of the Bicentennial, being denied rooms based on our skin color!

It took about an hour for all but one of the Province Polemarchs to arrive, and they all received the same treatment. Confirmation of our worst fears came when the last member of our group, Dave Thompkins, who could easily have passed for White, checked in without incident and was immediately given a key. When he turned and saw us, he waved and smiled warmly, assuming that we already had our rooms.

The front desk clerk, who was watching all of this, asked Dave, "Are you friends with those people? Are you with them?"

"Yes, of course," he said. "They're my fraternity brothers."

The clerk then literally snatched the key from his hands, and informed him that no room was available, after all.

As the rest of us burst out laughing, the ever-present smile on Dave's face quickly evaporated.

Meanwhile, one of the members of our group had placed a call to the most prominent Kappa in Philadelphia, H. H. Holloway, who was senior vice president and general counsel at the Federal Reserve Bank there. He was also the Grand Keeper of Records and Exchequers, the number four position in the fraternity, and later rose to become Grand Polemarch. It was Holloway's secretary who had made the hotel reservations for everyone.

In about half an hour, a profusely apologetic hotel manager appeared, to let us know that although our rooms had been given away, alternative accommodations at another hotel would be found for us that evening, and that our reservations at the Hilton would be honored for the remainder of our stay. The managerial staff then scrambled to find rooms for the dozen of us for that night. In the time that had passed, all of our rooms had been given away to White men, who apparently had had no reservations, but had just walked up to the front desk and asked for a room.

Clearly, the Hilton Hotel had been caught in a blatant case of racial discrimination. The next day, when we all gathered back at the Hilton, we discussed the possibility of a lawsuit, but instead accepted the apologies of the manager and a waiver of all our expenses for the remainder of the weekend, including for our bedrooms, our meeting rooms, and our food! I suspect that Brother Holloway may have obtained other compensation for our fraternity as well, although I was not privy to the details.

That experience was a reality check for me. I had graduated from one of the best law schools in the nation and was working successfully for a Fortune 500 corporation. Nevertheless, to some White people, I was a Black man, who could be denied access on the basis of my skin color. The outrageous conduct of that clerk reconfirmed my commitment to remain active in the NAACP to fight for civil rights.

One of the most difficult episodes during my tenure as Province Polemarch came when I had to engineer the ouster from a leadership position of a man I considered a friend. Stanley Hall, who had succeeded me as Polemarch of the Berkeley Alumni Chapter, was a brother whom I had initiated into the fraternity, nurtured, and encouraged to seek a leadership position. Because he was intelligent and likeable, he was elected without opposition. His tenure began smoothly enough, but after a few months the brothers who had supported his election began to see something in Stanley's management style that did not sit well with them. He had a "command and control" approach, an authoritarian leadership style that is a prescription for disaster in a volunteer organization, in which gentle persuasion and caring motivation are the keys to success. Stanley's inability to see any perspective other than his own was alienating him from the members.

After hearing the complaints and being asked to intervene, I spoke to Stanley as diplomatically as I could, although it was quickly apparent that he wasn't getting it. Basically, he said that he planned to continue to lead in any way that he deemed fit. In other words, he had an attitude of "My way or the highway."

Over the coming weeks, the members became more and more disgruntled, to the point where they decided to take a vote on whether Stanley should be removed from office. According to the fraternity's rules, removing an officer required a simple majority vote of the chapter's members, followed by a recommendation from the Province Polemarch—me— whose job it was to report to the fraternity's Grand Board of Directors, who would make the final decision. I soon learned that this procedure had never before been used against a sitting Chapter Polemarch.

Obviously, this was a delicate situation. Because I was required to make a recommendation on the issue, I recused myself from the chapter vote, during which the members chose decisively to remove Stanley. I made the recommendation to approve their request, and the national leadership accepted it. Stanley then stopped coming to meetings, and my relationship with him was certainly damaged, although we continued to associate outside the fraternity. It took many years before our friendship warmed up, but it eventually did, and we remained friends until his death in 2012.

Although I served as Polemarch of the Western Province of Kappa Alpha Psi from 1975 through 1979, I remained active in the National Bar Association too, as I had been since the start of my career at PG&E. In 1976, I was serving as assistant secretary of the NBA, when we were suddenly hit with a management crisis. Our Executive Director had made a financial mess of the national office in Washington, D.C., which put valuable government contracts at stake. When he was fired, the president of the NBA at the time, W. George Allen, sought a qualified replacement, and I recommended Elihu Harris, one of my Kappa brothers, whom I had mentored.

At the time, Elihu was working as a Legislative Assistant to Congresswoman Yvonne Burke of Los Angeles, so he knew his way around Capitol Hill, a big plus. I had known him since he was a student at California State University East Bay, formerly known as Cal State Hayward, where he pledged Kappa, and I was the undergraduate advisor to his chapter. Elihu went on to earn a master's degree from the University of California at Berkeley and a law degree from University of California at Davis. Although Elihu was admitted to the bar, he chose to enter the political arena instead. By the time I recommended him for the NBA job, he had established himself as a politically savvy young lawyer with a bright future.

When Elihu was invited to be interviewed by the NBA's Board of Governors, on which I sat, we flew together from the Bay Area on the same Delta Airlines flight to Washington. That gave me a chance to caution him to keep his "cool" during the interview, since I was fairly certain that some of the questions would irritate him. I knew Elihu well, and he didn't suffer fools lightly.

The interview began with routine questions about Elihu's education and employment. It was a "by the book" interview for the board members, some of whom had an unrealistic sense of self-importance. Just as I had feared, it was a frustrating experience for Elihu, especially when someone asked him, "Why do you want this job?"

Elihu erupted.

"I don't need this!" he exclaimed. "I don't need y'all! You need *me!*"

With that, he promptly stood up and left the room.

Many of the board members were floored. A few stunned eyes glanced over at me, since I was the one who had recommended Elihu for the position.

The truth was that the NBA really *did* need Elihu—or someone like him—who had connections with the federal government and a record of knowing how to get things done. People at several agencies had made it perfectly clear that we were in dire need of an Elihu, or our contracts would be at risk.

One such contract was with the Department of Housing and Urban Development. The NBA was obligated to conduct seminars around the country on topics related to fair housing laws. I argued that we should still pursue Elihu, but there was vehement disagreement on that among the members, most of whom felt that he was too arrogant. When the vote was taken, seventeen of the nineteen members voted against Elihu. Only George Allen and I were for him.

During the following week, George made calls related to the most critical contracts that the NBA was concerned about. When the government representatives asked if a replacement for the dismissed Executive Director had been hired, and whether Elihu had been selected, George stalled and called me.

"Bob," he said, "I don't care what it takes, but you must convince Elihu to take this job. If he doesn't, we're going out of business."

"George," I replied, "you're putting me in a difficult position. I have a candidate here who hasn't been offered the job…, who in fact stormed out of his interview. And you're asking me to get him back. And that's in the face of seventeen board members who hate the idea of hiring someone who's told them off."

"I'll take care of the board," he said. "You take care of Elihu."

Bringing the two sides together took a bit of diplomacy. When I reached out to Elihu, he initially told me that he thought I was crazy.

"How can I possibly work with *those* people?" he said. "They're arrogant and act as if I need the job."

When he finished venting, we had a calm, rational discussion about the future of the NBA, its importance to the Black community, and what was needed to make it a stronger, more viable advocate in the civil rights struggle. I appealed to his sense of duty to Black lawyers and judges, pointing out that the position would give him broader exposure, greatly enhancing his reputation nationally. In the end, Elihu agreed to serve as Executive Director for a limited time, two years at most. His goal was to put the NBA on the right track, and then leave.

Once the government agencies we were dealing with found out that Elihu had been chosen as Executive Director, our critical contracts were no longer in jeopardy. Indeed, Elihu brought in several new ones.

While Elihu was running the National Bar Association, I was serving as its assistant secretary. For a long time, Ben Travis had urged me to become part of the NBA's leadership. Before me, no lawyer from the West Coast had been an officer in the organization. However, Ben had a strategy. He wanted me to become assistant secretary and then expand the visibility of the position by using the same skills that I had demonstrated as his right-hand man when we were building the Charles Houston Law Club. Eventually, with support from the growing number of California lawyers, I became, with Ben's enthusiastic encouragement, the first West Coast attorney to ascend the NBA's ranks.

Since I was the only one who wanted the position, I ran uncontested. When I was elected assistant secretary in 1975, a highly capable female attorney from Chicago, Arnette Hubbard, was elected secretary. I had known Arnette for the past year and held her in high esteem. She was senior to me as a lawyer, having been in private practice for several years before I became a member of the bar. But both of us were ambitious.

Arnette assigned to me many of her duties as secretary, knowing that the effective use of my assistance would allow her to take on higher-profile projects. I even assumed the traditional role of secretary by taking the minutes at board meetings and ensuring that they were accurately recorded and distributed in a timely fashion.

Arnette delegated many responsibilities to me, and the harder I worked as assistant secretary, the more opportunities she had to be an outstanding secretary. We worked well together, complementing one another. Arnette was an excellent teacher and mentor, and helped me enormously to climb the leadership ladder. In 1980, she was elected the first (but not the last) female president of the NBA.

When I had been assistant secretary for about six months, Elihu Harris encouraged me to run for third vice president.

The NBA had a handful of vice presidents, so a new candidate for office would begin by running for fourth vice president. If he won against a large field of opponents from throughout the country, then later he would run for third vice president, and so on up the chain. Winning would be especially difficult for a candidate from the West Coast, since we were heavily outnumbered. The fourth vice president would normally come from New York, D.C., or somewhere in the Midwest.

Receiving the NBA's Highest Honor,
the C. Francis Stradford Award,
from Arnette Hubbard

Therefore, astute political tactician that he was, Elihu figured out that my best shot for becoming a vice president would be to disregard the customary procedure, which had never been done before. He recommended that I run for third vice president, thereby avoiding the melee of the race for the fourth position. It was a long shot, and I thought he was crazy, but Ben Travis agreed with Elihu's plan.

Although I had served as assistant secretary, I was not widely enough known by the national membership to be confident of being elected. Frankly, when I submitted my name for third vice president, some people thought I was foolish.

In 1976, the annual convention of the NBA was held in Houston, Texas. For a couple of months before we went there, Elihu, Ben, and I, along with some friends and supporters, launched a national campaign for my election. Our strategy was to use my contacts in Kappa Alpha Psi throughout the nation to garner support and energize the West Coast members as they had never been engaged before.

We succeeded. More than 150 lawyers from the West Coast descended on Houston, and, to the surprise of many, we beat the frontrunner, the current Fourth Vice President, Stuart Dunnings of Michigan. Stuart was a popular and seasoned lawyer, who had the support of the old establishment, but we were able to counter his following by organizing support from Arkansas and other Southern states, emphasizing that I was a native son.

With 55 percent of the vote, I became the third vice president of the National Bar Association. At that point, I was only thirty-two years old, and had been out of law school only four years. It was a tremendous victory for me, for Elihu, for Ben Travis, and for the West Coast region, which had never before been represented in the NBA's leadership.

In 1977, at our convention in New Orleans, I ran

unopposed for the position of second vice president. Then, at our convention in Hollywood, Florida, in 1978, I became president-elect (which was our name for first vice president). In 1979, Ben Travis's dream came to fruition, when I was installed as president of the NBA, the first ever from the West Coast.

But I've skipped over something important that happened before all this. Immediately after my stunning victory as third vice president at the 1976 NBA convention in Houston, the Black bar leaders in California envisioned that triumph as setting the stage for the formation of a statewide association of Black lawyers. Before I could take a victory lap, I was summoned to a meeting with Judge Ben Travis of the Alameda County Superior Court and Judge David F. Cunningham of the Los Angeles County Superior Court. Both had been instrumental in getting me elected and were excited about the potential of that. For them, it was far more than my being elected vice president of the NBA. Rather, in their view, it was clear and convincing evidence of the potential power of California lawyers to yield collective impact.

According to Ben and Dave's interpretation, the election was an indication that the time had come to establish a statewide association of Black lawyers in the state. At that time, the two major Black bar associations in California were the Charles Houston Bar in Oakland, which covered Northern California, and the John M. Langston Bar in Los Angeles, which covered Southern California. Ben was the guru of the former, while Dave was the guru of the latter. They saw my election as the catalyst for forming a statewide association of Black lawyers. Because I was president of the Charles Houston Bar and the third vice president of the NBA, I was expected to take the lead in laying the foundation for their newly envisioned statewide association.

Although several lawyers from Los Angeles were involved in the initial planning for that association, the key persons from Los Angeles, in addition to Dave, were Maxine F. Thomas (a past president of the Langston Bar) and Robert Roberson (then the current president). From Oakland, the key players, in addition to Ben, were George Holland (the NBA's director of Region IX), Thomas Broome, and Horace Wheatley. As the leader of the endeavor, I was tasked to draft the framework for the association, including its overall structure and bylaws.

Starting in the fall of 1976, I devoted an appreciable amount of my time to thinking through the concept of a statewide association, looking at other models around the country, and traveling between Oakland and Los Angeles. Once I had drafted the framework, and the leaders of the two associations had revised it, the name of the association took center stage. We finally agreed that it should be called the California Association of Black Lawyers (CABL). Our next critical step was to set the place and date for the association's launching—a critical aspect. To be a success, the conference had to draw at least 150 lawyers, the number that had traveled to Houston. A low attendance would not bode well for the new association.

Although we considered San Francisco and Oakland as potential venues, we decided that Los Angeles would most likely generate a greater attendance. To ensure unity, we had to introduce the organization with precision, so choosing an appropriate date was important. We finally determined, after checking everyone's schedule and the availability of rooms at the Los Angeles Airport Marriott Hotel, that Saturday, April 23, 1977, would be the best date.

Avoiding friction between the two sponsoring bar associations was a delicate matter, requiring them to feel that they were on an equal footing. Since I was the vice president of the NBA and the president of the Charles Houston Bar, I was selected to preside at the morning session to set the tone for the conference, while Robert Roberson would preside in the afternoon.

On the morning of April 23, with over 225 Black lawyers attending from throughout the state, I called the meeting to order at exactly 9:00 A.M., explaining the need for the association and the fundamental purpose of the conference, including what we expected to accomplish that day. Shortly after that, the members approved by a unanimous voice vote the official formation of the association, the agenda of the conference, the association's name, its bylaws, and other procedures.

Recognizing that we needed the support of most Black lawyers in the state, we had invited the leaders of the three other known Black lawyer groups in California to join us at the conference: Naomi Young (the president of the Black Women Lawyers of Northern California), Napoleon Jones (the president of the San Diego Black Lawyers), and Irma Brown (the president of the Southern California Chapter of Black Women Lawyers) were all invited and given an opportunity to speak about the need for the new association. In addition, the presence of nationally known Black lawyers, such as Willie Brown, Elihu Harris, and William (Billy) Hunter, as well as many Black judges, gave credence to the purpose of the conference.

A few weeks before the conference, Governor Jerry Brown had appointed Alameda County Superior Court Judge Wiley W. Manuel as the first Black justice of the California Supreme Court. That was an unexpected bonus for us, adding a huge incentive for attendance, since Justice Manuel, who was sworn in on April 21, just two days prior to our conference, had already agreed to be our keynote speaker.

Inviting Justice Manuel to our conference, as well as Governor Brown, proved to be a wise strategy that generated wide interest, not only from lawyers but also from the media. According to the *Los Angeles Sentinel*, "Some of the nation's most prominent Black attorneys and judges were present to witness the birth of the California Association of Black Lawyers."

Following Justice Manuel's speech at our luncheon, the afternoon session commenced, with Roberson presiding. Most of the afternoon was filled with panel discussions on issues such as affirmative action and the need for more Black judges. The final business matter of the day was the election of the first CABL president, who would lead the new organization into the future—a responsibility not to be taken lightly.

Feeling that it was essential to select a leader of impeccable credentials, California's most prominent politician, Willie Brown, thought he had the answer. Before the election, he had asked me if I were interested in being president. I assured him that, as president of the Charles Houston Bar and vice president of the NBA, I already had a full plate.

Willie then asked Donald McCullum, one of the founders of the Charles Houston Bar, if he were interested. Don, a noted

NAACP lawyer and civil rights activist, who had also served as Berkeley's first Black city attorney, had come prepared for the offer, and eagerly consented. However, Willie's nomination of Don caught his opponent from Southern California, Maxine F. Thomas (whose interest in being president was well known) by surprise.

With Willie Brown (center) and Elihu Harris

Prior to the election, there had been nothing to divide the two bar associations. But now we had a prominent member of the Charles Houston Bar running against a prominent member of the Langston Bar. Nevertheless, thanks to Willie's political astuteness, a compromise was found: Don was elected the first president of CABL, and Maxine was elected president-elect! Never underestimate Willie Brown's ability to find political solutions where there appear to be none!

As a result of CABL's birth and the political pressure it was able to exert, Governor Brown appointed an unprecedented number of Black judges, including Don McCullum. Moreover, almost immediately, CABL began to take on some of the most important issues in California, including the administration of the prison system, support of affirmative action, the filing of amicus briefs, and opposition to the rise of the Ku Klux Klan in the state.

Regarding the Klan, perhaps the most memorable moment for me personally occurred when CABL gained national attention in the early 1980s for sponsoring state legislation to curb the Klan's rising activities. Worst of all, three young White men, allegedly Klan members, had gone deer hunting in Chico, and after failing to find a deer to kill, they decided to hunt for and kill a Black man instead. Outraged by that senseless murder, which occurred right on the city streets, CABL asked me to draft language, which was then submitted to California's Senate by Diane Watson (who later became a member of the U.S. Congress), to curtail the advocacy of imminent violence. The bill sparked national attention, even in the *New York Times*. Although the legislation was vigorously opposed at the time by the ACLU and other similar groups, CABL refused, in the face of enormous pressure, to back down. And today, California Code of Civil Procedure 527.7 resonates as a shining example of CABL's tenacity—a history unknown to many.

19

Work-Life Balance

*Seems like God don't see fit to give the Black man
nothing but dreams—but He did give us children to
make them dreams seem worthwhile.*

—Lorraine Hansberry

During that first decade of my professional growth, my time
was clearly dominated by my work and volunteer endeavors. I
was as driven as an athlete with eyes on the Olympics—driven
to succeed against all odds, driven to steadily move up, driven
to seize and exploit every opportunity that presented itself. It
wasn't just for me. I had children. What I did, I did for them,
too.

My day began at 5:00 A.M. Before 6:00, dressed typically
in a polyester suit and wide necktie, as was fashionable then,
I moved swiftly out the door and headed for an AC Transit
bus for a 35-minute ride to downtown San Francisco from my
home in Richmond. (This was before Bay Area Rapid Transit,
better known as BART, began operating.) Once I got to the
office, I read the newspaper when I could, but mostly I began
working on my cases right away, spending considerable time
in the law library doing research for Dick. I tried, when I didn't

have other commitments, to be home by 5:30 or 6:00 P.M. to have dinner with my family. But those other engagements often took priority.

My kids, Tony and Regina, were eight and six respectively when I started at PG&E in September 1972. Looking back, I clearly didn't spend as much time with them as I should have, but I did spend a fair amount of time, especially with Tony. He and I would occasionally go fishing with my friend Lester, after whom Tony (actually Anthony Lester Harris) was named, and I would occasionally take him out on other father-son excursions, including Little League. Esther, my wife at that time, who was a schoolteacher, was the one who spent the most time with him and Regina on their homework. I often went to parent-teacher conferences and other school events, but Esther was the primary leader in their academic education, which was okay with her because she supported my ambitions.

However, by 1977, my marriage was troubled, for many other reasons. My own maturity or lack thereof was a factor, I'm sure. When our kids were thirteen and eleven, Esther and I separated, and I became a weekend dad. But I can't truthfully say that I saw them every weekend, or even nearly every other weekend.

To be honest, I cannot say that I had any work-life balance in those early years, because the very concept didn't even exist at that time. I was a young man, and like other men of my age and generation, I believed that my primary responsibility was to provide materially for my family—a roof over their heads, clothes on their backs, and food on the table. I was committed to establishing myself professionally, believing that whatever benefits I reaped would benefit my family.

In hindsight, I have few regrets about my life, but not spending more time with Tony and Regina is surely one of them.

I do, however, have some very fond memories of time spent together with them. In 1980, for example, I took them with me to the National Bar Association's annual convention in Dallas, where I presided as president. Before arriving at the convention, we stopped in Arkadelphia to visit my parents, which I think served to root my kids in a positive way.

20

Connections Pay Dividends

I've got to keep on pushing (mmm-hmm)
I can't stop now
Move up a little higher
Some way, somehow

—Tevin Campbell

After five years in the legal department at PG&E, I was promoted to Senior Counsel. I had mastered the basics, and my new title suggested that I was considered proficient by my peers. My career was moving in the right direction, and my work in the community served to enhance my stature in the company. It looked good that I had obtained leadership roles in the Charles Houston Bar Association, the National Bar Association, and Kappa Alpha Psi, which served to cement the general feeling that the company had made a good choice in hiring me. In addition, I was making valuable contacts that proved useful to PG&E. But the efforts to achieve all that would backfire on me.

As one example of how my contacts helped PG&E, I was able to arrange a simple but vital phone call for the company.

In the mid-1980s, PG&E was frustrated in its efforts to get permits for the Diablo Canyon Nuclear Power Plant, which was under construction in San Luis Obispo. This was the single most important issue facing the company at the time, and delays were causing the costs to skyrocket. PG&E, which had an extensive government relations system with offices in Sacramento, was nevertheless unable to connect with Governor George Deukmejian's office—specifically, with his legal affairs secretary.

As it happened, that secretary was a Black lawyer whom I knew through the California Association of Black Lawyers (CABL), of which I was one of the principal founders. In April 1977, some 200 lawyers from around the state attended our first annual meeting, with the purpose of uniting Black attorneys to establish effective networks to ensure that our voices were heard on issues of concern to us. One of the bright young lawyers I had met through CABL and the NBA was Vance Raye, a rising star who was well-respected in the legal profession. A former member of the California State Attorney General's office, Vance was now the governor's legal affairs secretary, the key advisor on all legal matters, including issues related to Diablo Canyon.

Early one morning, PG&E's general counsel, Malcolm Furbush, dropped by my office to discuss an issue concerning the final phase of the permit process for Unit 1 of the nuclear power plant.

After nervously explaining the problem, he said, "Bob, I heard you know the governor's legal affairs secretary."

My first thoughts were, *Who told you, and how did they know?*

"Yes, I do," I responded. "He's an old friend of mine."

Malcolm then explained that, for some reason, Vance was not returning PG&E's phone calls, and it was urgent that they talk with him immediately. By now, it was becoming clear why the general counsel was in my office at 7:30 in the morning. Obviously, he viewed me as the key to contacting Vance Raye. I played it cool, explaining how I knew him and the nature of our relationship. I wanted the general counsel to fully appreciate the value of my external networks, since I was aware that there were grumblings from some about my outside activities.

Sensing that he had gotten my point, I said, "Malcolm, is there something you think I can do to assist in this matter?"

Without hesitation, he blurted out, "Can you call Vance and explain the urgency of why we need to speak with him immediately?"

I deliberately hesitated for a moment.

"Well, I suspect he's very busy on other matters," I said, "but I'll give him a call later this morning to see why he hasn't returned your calls."

Malcolm was happy.

When I phoned the legal affairs secretary's office, around 10:30 A.M., his assistant said he was not available, but she would let him know that I wanted to speak to him. About thirty minutes later, Vance returned my call. After exchanging greetings, I explained why PG&E had been making urgent attempts to reach him. He indicated that he had received their calls, but saw no reason to respond immediately to them. From the tone in his voice, I got the feeling that he was enjoying not returning their calls, in order to let them feel the heat, so to speak.

After a while, he said, "Bob, if you think it's important for me to return their calls, I'll do so today."

"I would personally appreciate your doing so."

"Consider it done."

A few minutes later, I was in Malcolm's office with the good news. He was delighted. As promised, the legal affairs secretary called that afternoon.

As I noted above, there had occasionally been some grumbling in the legal department about my outside activities, and this incident did not quell that. Eventually, someone complained. Envy is rampant in any competitive environment; in this case, one of my colleagues objected to our boss about my outside work. He was particularly concerned about the reimbursement of my travel expenses, perceiving them as additional compensation. He must have made a strong case, because our boss called me in to inform me that those expenses would no longer be reimbursed.

Since that pronouncement caught me completely off-guard, I didn't know quite how to react initially, so I consulted one of my mentors, Dick Clarke. Still informally known as "King Richard," Dick was no longer in the legal department, but had been promoted to president, and was on the way to becoming PG&E's CEO. He was clearly the right person to seek advice from, because he had always been supportive of my "outside" work. Indeed, he encouraged it and had always seen to it that my travel expenses were paid. As a matter of fact, when I became president of the NBA, he assigned a full-time secretary to attend solely to my national bar work.

Dick took the position that it helped to create a public image of PG&E as supportive of pro bono work and community involvement, which was true. We agreed that the best way to handle this delicate situation would be to plead my case to my boss's boss, the general counsel, Malcolm Furbush. When I did just that, he asked me to draft a memorandum outlining the circumstances under which lawyers in our department would be reimbursed for travel expenses related to outside activities.

Naturally, I drafted guidelines that would allow me to continue to be reimbursed. When Malcolm accepted my guidelines, telling me that they were totally reasonable, he had them distributed to the legal department, much to the ire of the complaining attorney. (I knew all this from my secretary.) As it turned out, no one else in the legal department but me ever came close to meeting the guidelines.

From that episode, I learned that any setback had to be taken in stride. As someone once said, a setback is nothing more than a setup for a comeback.

21

May It Please the Court

*I am invisible, understand, simply because people
refuse to see me.*

—Ralph Ellison

Only two percent of lawyers in the country get the chance
to argue a case before the United States Supreme Court. That
opportunity is usually won through lengthy battles in the lower
courts. In my case, however, the battles were as much outside
of legal arenas as inside. My case was a long shot, and so was
I.

In the early 1980s, several states had passed legislation that
required utilities to include in their billing envelopes messages
from consumer groups that were opposed to their rates or
policies. In our case, the order had come from the California
Public Utilities Commission (CPUC), telling PG&E that it
had to include messages from TURN (Toward Utility Rate
Normalization) in its monthly billing envelopes.

PG&E was reluctantly prepared to obey the order, since
it felt it had no choice. Nevertheless, before the order came
down, I had written several legal memoranda, arguing that

the anticipated order was unconstitutional because it violated corporate free speech. For the most part, my advice had been discarded because most of the leading legal scholars in the nation believed that utility companies had no constitutional right to object to this requirement.

I lobbied my bosses to challenge the CPUC's order, and they ultimately requested a formal hearing before the commission. However, as the consulting legal scholars had predicted, the commission ruled against us. But I wasn't finished with this matter.

When the company began making plans to comply with the order, I strongly objected. Regardless of what the legal scholars had said, I was confident that we could ultimately win the case, if given an opportunity to appeal the decision of the CPUC. At first, no one paid any attention to me, thinking I was being ridiculous. If we appealed, they thought, it would be a waste of resources. Because we had no appellate attorneys on our staff, we would have to hire outside counsel, whose fees would be astronomical.

On that score, they were absolutely right. The fees of the big law firms would be prodigious. But I had a different strategy. Forget the big law firms! As a staff lawyer, *I* could appeal the decision. To my associates, that idea was ludicrous. After all, the case had not been presented to the commission by me, but by Peter Hanschen, the regular attorney who handled those affairs. Therefore, why would I be chosen to take on the appeal? Furthermore, I had no appellate experience, so it made no sense to allow a rookie to pursue a case that legal scholars said could not be won.

Unwilling to give up, since I strongly believed I was right,

I approached Malcolm Furbush and Peter Hanschen, who had read the several legal memoranda I had written on the matter. They listened to my reasons why I thought the case could be won on appeal, but they remained unconvinced, insinuating that pursuing a dead-end appeal might embarrass the company.

Nevertheless, I kept arguing until Malcolm finally said he would allow me to pursue the appeal if he could get PG&E's CEO and management team to agree. He didn't feel comfortable, he said, proceeding with the appeal without the sanction of PG&E's leadership, because he knew that the CPUC's orders were only very rarely overruled by the California Supreme Court.

"Bob," he said, "you need to know that a huge risk is being taken by appealing the CPUC's decision."

"I agree," I said. "But I still think we can win."

Now, I had already thought this thing out and had a strategy. Understanding the financial and political risks, I explained to Malcolm that I didn't expect to win at the California Supreme Court. Once denied by it, however, I planned to petition the U.S. Supreme Court to accept the case for review. Eventually, after deep skepticism, Malcolm agreed with me, and was successful in getting PG&E's top leadership to approve my plan.

As expected, my appeal to the California Supreme Court was promptly rejected, with no written opinion explaining why. The next step presented a major obstacle that I'm sure made Malcolm have second thoughts about having agreed to the appeal. Someone pointed out to him that the U.S. Supreme Court had *never* consented to review a case that did not have a written opinion from a lower court. Malcolm probably thought that I had pushed him into a corner without him fully realizing the obstacles we faced. I assured him we could convince the High Court to review the case, despite this obstacle. I'm not sure if I really believed what I was saying, but by then I was obsessed with the belief that the case was winnable, which was probably clouding my judgment.

After thorough legal research, I discovered that it was true that the Court had never accepted a case for review when, as in our case, there was no written opinion from a lower court. Thus, we were asking the Court to review a case based solely on an opinion of an administrative body, the CPUC.

Having put his credibility on the line, Malcolm allowed me to move forward, since only my salary, as a staff attorney, would be at stake, and therefore no costly outside counsel fees would be incurred. Moreover, he permitted me to devote almost all of my time to writing the Jurisdictional Statement (brief), which was the sole document the Court would rely on to decide whether to accept the case for review. Malcolm only made one stipulation: I had to do all the research and writing myself. In other words, I was "on my own."

Actually, that was fine with me.

As I began the required rigorous research and brief writing, a health issue suddenly emerged that created a crisis for me just when I didn't need one. In late summer 1984, my stomach began aching from time to time for no apparent reason. At first, my physician, Dr. Zealous Wiley, a noted gastroenterologist who was also my friend and Kappa brother, said it was probably just bowel irritation, which could be caused by certain foods or any of a number of other causes. In any case, the pain persisted, becoming more intense and regular.

Zealous ordered a CAT scan of my stomach to ensure that nothing unusual was happening there. When the results of the scan, which was performed at Marshall Hale Hospital in San Francisco, were returned, they showed an unusual mass at the top of my pancreas. Clearly, this was not good news. Such a mass, I was informed, usually meant pancreatic cancer, one of the deadliest forms. Once diagnosed, it usually, but not always, means a remaining life span of six months or less. I was just forty years old. Was I dying?

Although Zealous assured me that it was highly unlikely that I had cancer, I was skeptical of his assurances.

"Why are you so optimistic," I asked, "in view of the results of the CAT scan?"

"Bob," he said, "I can't argue with the results of the CAT scan, but I do know a cancer patient when I see one, and you don't fit the model."

By now, perhaps because of my fears, my stomach pains disappeared, and I oddly felt fine physically. Emotionally, however, I was a wreck. Zealous ordered further tests, one of which was a painful spinal tap because my white blood cell count was low, one indicator of cancer. That was a nightmare, but Zealous kept shaking his head when I saw him next.

"There's something wrong here," he said.

At times like that, it is helpful to have an advocate, and I lived with an ideal one: I was married to a doctor.

I had met Glenda Newell after separating from my first wife in 1977. We had met a year later, during the summer of 1978, while Glenda was a medical student at the University of Cincinnati, working as an assistant for her uncle, who was a physician in San Francisco. After she graduated in 1979, she returned to San Francisco for an internship at Mt. Zion Hospital and then went into private practice. After we dated for a while, we became engaged in 1983 and set a wedding date for March 17, 1984, in Winston-Salem, North Carolina, where Glenda had grown up. Her parents were college professors at Winston-Salem State University, and, in addition, her mother was an elected member of the city council.

Cutting the Wedding Cake

More than four hundred guests attended our wedding reception in the city's convention center, many coming from other parts of the country. My longtime friend Elihu Harris, who at the time was a leader in the California State Legislature, served as my best man. Ted Newman, who was the Chief Judge of the District of Columbia Court of Appeals, was a groomsman, along with my mentor, Alameda County Superior

Court Judge Benjamin Travis, and another close friend, noted Oakland civil rights attorney John Burris.

So, when I had my health scare, Glenda was in direct contact with my doctor. After discussing my case for a while, they concluded that there might be something wrong with the CAT scan machine itself. When Glenda anxiously called several experts on CAT scans, she was advised to have a second scan at UC San Francisco Hospital, which used a different brand of machine than the one at Marshall Hale. Zealous concurred.

On the day of the new exam, Glenda accompanied me to the hospital. As I entered the machine, I prayed. Within a minute or so after the test was done, the radiologist and Glenda were by my side, both of them with big smiles on their faces.

"There's no mass or anything else on your pancreas," the radiologist said.

All this anxiety had been created by a defective machine!

It was like a voice from heaven. I was fully energized again and ready to take on the appeal.

For the next three months, starting in September 1984, I spent most of my legal time wrestling with the appeal, researching every related case I could find and crafting every conceivable argument that made sense to me. Since my reputation at the company was at stake, I was driven. Finally, on Christmas Eve, I submitted the brief to the United States Supreme Court. Recognizing that it was highly unlikely that the Court would accept jurisdiction, I knew I had done my best, and there was nothing else I could do except try to enjoy the Christmas season with my family, which I did.

After the New Year, I returned to my regular duties in the legal department, relieved that I could finally free my mind of First Amendment theories and detailed constitutional law cases. Nevertheless, I was never really free of the nagging thought that I might have used stronger arguments in my brief.

Then, one morning, about 6:30, the telephone in my office rang.

"May I speak to Mister Harris?" the caller asked.

"This is Mister Harris," I said.

The caller, who then identified himself as a reporter, asked, "What do you think of the Supreme Court's decision to hear PG&E's envelope case?"

For a second, I couldn't process what he had just said.

"What do you mean?"

"The Supreme Court has decided to hear the PG&E case."

"That's great!" I said. "But I'll have to call you back later, because I'm not prepared to talk at this moment."

I didn't bother to tell him this, but the communications department at PG&E required its approval for all interviews related to the company.

As soon as I hung up the phone, I headed to the general counsel's office. His door was open, and I raced right in.

"The Supreme Court," I said, "has accepted our case!"

"How do you know?"

"Because a reporter in Washington, D.C., from the Associated Press just called for my reaction."

Malcolm jumped out of his seat, happier than I had ever seen him before. PG&E was going to the U.S. Supreme Court, and I was the hero of the legal department. Unfortunately, my jubilant mood didn't last long.

The question eventually turned to who would argue the case on our behalf. Although I had written the persuasive brief, no one but me thought for a moment that I should be the one to go to Washington to argue the case before the Court. The conversations always began with weighing which of the various prominent law firms with Supreme Court experience we should retain. No eyes turned to me, even as a remote possibility. I now knew what it felt like to be Ralph Ellison's invisible man.

In the end, I was asked to assist in selecting the appropriate law firm to handle our case. The selection process soon captured the attention of PG&E's chairman of the board, Fred Mielke, who was an alumnus of our department and of Stanford Law School. Fred insisted that Professor William Cohen from Stanford, who was an expert on constitutional law, should make the recommendation.

Professor Cohen and I reviewed a number of law firms, many of which had earlier advised PG&E that there was little possibility that the Supreme Court would accept the case for review. Some were even firms that had refused to extend an offer of employment to me as I desperately sought a position in my last year of law school. Now many of these law firms were beating on the doors of PG&E to argue the case. Professor Cohen's nod was the key.

After I sent him all the briefs and other materials for his review, I drove down to his office on the Stanford campus several times to discuss the merits of the case. It was like going back to law school, so I took the opportunity to have a bit of argumentative fun. It was clear that the distinguished professor was somewhat taken aback at first by my approach and knowledge of the complex issues, but our exchanges were vigorous.

After we concluded our discussions, I scheduled a time for us to meet with PG&E's general counsel, Malcolm Furbush, and a team of lawyers he had assembled. The meeting began with Professor Cohen discussing the case and its merits, including the points of law that suggested we might be able to win. At the end of a lively hour of back and forth, the professor did something that no one saw coming.

Looking over at Malcolm, he asked, "Do you want to win this case?"

Furbush looked confused.

"Of *course*, we want to win," Malcolm said. "That's why we have *you* here. To tell us which law firm can argue the case and win it."

Professor Cohen looked Malcolm squarely in the eye.

"If you really want to win this case, I only know one lawyer who can do it for you."

Then he pointed at me!

"That young man. If you want to win this case before the U.S. Supreme Court, he's the one who is going to have to argue it for you."

I could see the look on everyone's face—a combination of envy, disappointment, and stunned surprise. I suspect that any one of the lawyers in that conference room could have been knocked over by a feather. Never in their wildest dreams did they—or I, for that matter—think that Professor Cohen was going to recommend *me*.

Malcolm smiled and said he concurred. But then he let me know that he would have to consult with Fred Mielke. Even with Professor Cohen's recommendation and his own support, the decision was not a slam dunk. However, after a lengthy review that lasted several days, the board agreed to let me argue the case, with the stipulation that Professor Cohen would continue to serve as a consultant.

Soon after that, the team of lawyers who had been in the meeting with Professor Cohen began scrambling to get recognition. They wanted to be named as counsels who would be listed under the general counsel's name and my name on the brief. However, as I went to work on the case, I was unconcerned with the office politics. But after I sent the first draft around to the team, they came back with all kinds of uninformed suggestions. I was open to having their names on the brief, but not to having their irrelevant contributions to the content.

That's when I realized that I had a problem. I would be heading nowhere with this case if I had to take positions that demonstrated no idea of the issues, much less how to deal with them. Therefore, I immediately headed to Malcolm's office to let him know that this team approach was not going to work.

He was very attentive to my arguments, and in the end agreed that only two names would appear on the brief—his as general counsel and mine—with Professor Cohen as consultant on the final content. If there were any disagreements over the content of the brief, my decision would be final. Clearly, Malcolm put absolute confidence in my ability.

When I think back on how I handled the selection process, I can see now how *not* fighting was the winning strategy. I can't say that I planned it that way, but I can say that I played my cards well. If I had gone to my superiors in the legal department and tried to persuade them that I should be the one to argue the case, I would have lost. How could the company have trusted me to argue a case before the nation's highest court when I had such limited trial experience and virtually no appellate experience? But I proved to Professor Cohen, one of the most brilliant constitutional law experts in the nation, that I had the most thorough knowledge of the case and the clearest understanding of the various issues it raised, and he fought my battles for me as my champion.

After I had dutifully filed all the final written briefs, it was time to prepare for the oral argument. What would I say? How I would say it? And, most critically, how would I respond to the questions I anticipated would be posed by the nine Justices? Like an ambitious actor about to take on his first leading role, I knew I needed to rehearse, so I reached out to my alma mater for assistance.

The dean of Boalt Hall at the time was Jesse H. Choper, who, like Professor Cohen, was a nationally recognized constitutional law scholar. I had known and admired Professor Choper from my days as a student, so I was very pleased that he agreed to help me. I asked for a panel of three law professors of his choosing to read my briefs and act as judges as I argued the case before them. In law school, we called that moot court.

My secretary sent the briefs to all the professors selected for the panel and scheduled a date for the moot court. On the appointed date, I went to the law school to face this distinguished panel of learned professors, to test myself, and to see if I could defend the position that I planned to argue in Washington. The moot court was organized in the moot courtroom, as if it were truly a case before the High Court. That meant I would be limited to exactly thirty minutes to make my oral argument— for which I felt prepared.

Prior to the moot court, Dean Choper had already given me his assessment: the briefs were well-drafted, he said. But, given his understanding of the case and the issues, he didn't believe that I would get the Supreme Court to rule in my favor. I certainly valued his feedback, which probably toughened me for the moot court. Perhaps I boxed just a little bit more aggressively than I would have otherwise. In any case, the professors asked tough questions, and I felt comfortable with my responses.

After the session, I met informally with the panel for feedback. They were quite cordial and frank with me. While my briefs had allowed them to remain skeptical, they said, my oral arguments had substantially shifted their conclusions. If they had had the power to vote, they told me, my oral argument would have persuaded them to vote in my favor! That encouraged me enormously.

Every year, the Supreme Court begins to hear cases on the first Monday in October. In 1985, the first Monday was the seventh, and my case was scheduled to be heard the following day, the eighth. I arrived in D.C. on the Friday before the hearing.

Three weeks before my arrival, I had contacted Ted Newman, who was the Chief Judge of the District of Columbia Court of Appeals, because he was one of my Kappa Alpha Psi brothers, a fellow member of the National Bar Association, and a friend whom I greatly respected. In fact, he had been a groomsman at my wedding to Glenda. My secretary had sent him the briefs that I had submitted to the Supreme Court, and he had agreed to review them.

I had expected that Ted and I would meet informally in

his chambers, where he would pose some tough questions—hopefully some new ones—after we discussed my oral arguments. However, when I arrived, the court building was closed, since it was a Saturday. Nevertheless, there was a marshal at the door who was expecting me, and he escorted me to Ted's chambers.

When I got there, Ted greeted me warmly, but instead of ushering me to a cushy armchair for what I anticipated would be a serious chat, he did something that puzzled me. Without explanation, he walked to his closet, from which he extracted his black robe, and after putting it on, he asked me to follow him. We went through several doorways leading to the Appellate Court, where he presided. Once we got inside, Ted walked up to the bench, took his seat as Chief Judge, and instructed me to go to the lectern to argue my case.

That caught me completely by surprise. I had envisioned brotherly guidance and did not at all expect to be standing all alone at a lectern in an empty courtroom, quizzically looking up at Ted's firm, impenetrable stare as he shifted to his very impressive judicial voice.

"Mister Harris," he said, "you may proceed!"

Obviously, it wasn't Ted any longer whom I was addressing that Saturday. I was sparring with Chief Judge Theodore R. Newman, Jr., who proceeded to give me the most excruciating examination that I had received thus far. Three days away from the point-of-no-return moment when I would be arguing my case, here I was, sweating profusely under my friend's grueling scrutiny.

In fact, Judge Newman shook the very foundation of my case, speaking to me from the bench as if he doubted every word that I was uttering. I was left reeling from his questioning, and he let me know later with a devilish smile that he had enjoyed every moment of my agony. He also pronounced that he thought my arguments were without merit, and that the Justices would reject them. Simply put, he said, I was on the wrong side of the issue.

As we parted ways, he assured me that he would be in the courtroom to witness my oral arguments on Tuesday afternoon. Despite what he thought about the merits of the case, he told me that he was fully confident that I was more than sufficiently ready to argue it.

On Tuesday, October 8, 1985, I entered the awe-inspiring, four-story, neoclassical U.S. Supreme Court Building in the morning to watch the first two cases of the day, so that I could get a better feel for what was coming my way. The courtroom was not packed that morning, but after lunch when I returned, it was a very different scene. The inner circle of the first floor, where members of the bar sit, was filled with Black lawyers and judges from the National Bar Association, who had come from throughout the D.C. area to hear me argue the case, and they surely provided a helpful measure of comfort to me. I suspect that there were probably more Black attorneys than the Court had ever seen before to hear a corporate case.

In addition, there were many White corporate lawyers from across the nation who were eager to hear the arguments made in defense of a corporation's right to Free Speech under the First Amendment. Clearly, there was keen interest in this case. Nearly fifty friend-of-the-court briefs had been filed with the Court on both sides of the issue.

There was also especially keen interest by some of my

family members, who were watching attentively from the gallery. They included my wife, Glenda, my son, Tony, who was now a student at Howard University, and Glenda's parents, George Fisher Newell and Virginia Kimbrough Newell, both professors at Winston-Salem State University.

All eyes were on me and my colleagues as we took our assigned seats in the courtroom. The way it works in the U.S. Supreme Court is that each side is allowed three lawyers to sit at the table directly in front of the Justices. The lawyer who will argue the case—in this case, me—is expected to sit in the far right chair facing the Justices.

When the three of us approached the table—two White men (Malcolm Furbush, the general counsel; and Peter Hanschen, the original attorney for the case) and I—there were some soft murmurs as I occupied the arguing chair. For a lawyer, this was huge. As I looked up at the Justices, I thought that I saw Associate Justice Thurgood Marshall give me a nod, a smile, and a look that said, "Isn't this interesting?" Marshall was an icon for Black lawyers and Black people in general. Not only was he the first Black United States Supreme Court Justice, but he had successfully argued one of the most historically significant cases of importance to Black people, Brown vs. Board of Education.

At 2:00 P.M., Chief Justice Warren E. Burger called the Court to order. Then he announced, "We will now hear the case of Pacific Gas and Electric Company versus the Public Utilities Commission of the State of California."

Associate Justice Harry Blackmon immediately recused himself from hearing the case, without explaining why, so now we had only eight Black robes.

By the time I rose to argue the case, I felt totally ready. I walked calmly to the lectern and without trembling or showing any signs of fear in my voice, I said, "Mister Chief Justice Burger, may it please the Court," which is the customary way all attorneys begin their arguments at the U.S. Supreme Court. As I gazed firmly into the faces of all the Justices, one by one, I stated my name and said that I was representing PG&E. But I hadn't spoken much more than a minute when I was interrupted by Associate Justice William Rehnquist.

"Where did you get the notion," he asked, "that the First Amendment applies to a corporation in a negative sense?"

That was the icebreaker. I knew that Justice Rehnquist, given his past decisions, was not likely to rule in my favor. Here was the first challenge, meant to derail me, but it did not. I smiled at Justice Rehnquist and turned to stare directly into the face of Justice Lewis Powell.

"I got that notion," I said, "from Justice Powell."

In a 1978 decision, First National Bank of Boston vs. Bellotti, 435 U.S. 765, Justice Powell had written that corporations were protected by the First Amendment—specifically, that they had the right to expend money in elections on the basis of free speech. So, I argued that First Amendment free speech rights should also apply to corporations in the negative sense, which protects the right to speak and the right *not* to speak.

"A utility," I argued, "should not be compelled to carry in a billing envelope a message that reason tells it, it should not carry."

I knew from my research that winning would require getting the votes of Justices William Brennan and Thurgood Marshall, the two most liberal Justices on the Court. Even

Professor Cohen thought that was unlikely. My strategy was to make a forceful play to them during my argument that, by not voting in favor of PG&E, they would be inconsistent with prior decisions of theirs, in which they had expressed tremendous disdain for the government deciding who can and who cannot speak.

I made certain that I cited *all* of the cases they had ruled on regarding that issue. So, when Chief Justice Burger asked me who would decide which organizations would get to insert their messages in PG&E's billing envelopes, I was ready. Looking squarely at Marshall and Brennan, I blurted out, with my voice rising, "This can *only* be done by the government picking and choosing who gets to speak! As you know, Justices Brennan and Marshall have consistently stated in numerous cases that government has no business picking and choosing who can speak!"

With that single statement, I was confident that those two Justices would weigh my argument heavily.

The rest of my thirty minutes were saturated with questions from the other Justices.

At the Supreme Court

According to the Associated Press, the oral arguments were the most animated in recent Court history. What I remember vividly was that, during the oral arguments, Justice Sandra Day O'Connor, the first female Justice appointed to the Court, misspoke. While questioning the opposing counsel, who argued after me, she referred to him as "Mister Harris."

I silently thought, *I must have made a good impression on her. Why else would she still be thinking of me?*

Apparently, I didn't make such a good impression on Sylvia Siegel, the Executive Director of TURN, the organization that was the original plaintiff against PG&E, who rushed up to me as I left the courtroom.

"Mister Harris," she said, in a loud voice, "how *could* you stand up there, defending PG&E?"

Without thinking, I quickly responded, "Because PG&E is right!"

She stared at me in silence for at least five seconds. During that tense time, Glenda, who was by my side, was not at all pleased. As it turned out, her stern glance was enough to scare Sylvia off.

As Glenda and I flew back to California, I didn't expect the Court's decision to be handed down before March 1986. Therefore, when I received a phone call from an Associated Press reporter on February 25th, I was startled.

"Would you like to comment on the Supreme Court decision?" he asked.

"What decision?"

"PG&E won in the Supreme Court."

As soon as I got the details, I ran to Malcolm Furbush's office with the news. He was so ecstatic that he literally picked me up in the air! Later, the whole legal department celebrated at lunch and then at a bar after work.

It turned out that my hunch that I had persuaded Justices Marshall and Brennan was correct, for they gave me the crucial fourth and fifth votes needed to win the case!

The decision had national implications, so there were many requests to me for interviews and numerous speaking engagements—as well as an unexpected check for me from PG&E for $20,000!

At the annual review of Supreme Court cases held in Washington that September in 1986, Dean Choper, who was one of the two reviewers, along with Professor Lawrence Tribe of Harvard Law School, had the task of presenting my case, which he had told me I would never win. As I sat in the audience that morning, I eagerly awaited Dean Choper's remarks. After describing the issues in the case and critiquing the Court's decision, he surprised me. Admitting that he had predicted the Court would *not* uphold PG&E's position, he informed the audience that the lawyer who argued the case was a former student at his law school.

At that point, he said, "I would like to introduce to you the lawyer who won this case…. Bob Harris, please stand!"

Of the more than 200 lawyers present, I was the only Black lawyer in the room. As the applause faded, I felt a sense of victory with Dean Choper's acknowledgment of my win, despite his prediction of defeat. It was a great day!

That Supreme Court decision was the high point of my legal career. Where could I go from there?

22

Moving Down to Move Up

*After climbing a great hill, one only finds that there
are many more hills to climb.*

—Nelson Mandela

A couple of years after the Supreme Court ruling, I began
to express a serious desire to advance within the company, a
move that would involve leaving the legal department, where,
aside from the position of general counsel, there were no other
ways to become an officer.

By then, Malcolm Furbush had retired, and the general
counsel was Howard Golub, who was a supporter and friend
of mine. One day, Howard asked me to come into his office
to have a frank conversation about whether I really wanted to
leave the legal department to focus on the business side of the
company.

"I really want to give you candid feedback, Bob," he
began. "While I don't agree with them, others in management
have a specific reason for why they will oppose you going to
the business side of the company."

Then he cited, of all things, my diction.

"Your Southern type accent," he said, "is not representative of what they would like in an officer."

What?!

I was puzzled and more than a little angry. My diction had given me a voice that was sufficient to win a Supreme Court case for the company! Furthermore, I had spoken on numerous occasions, including on television, in which I had credibly represented PG&E. In none of those many different situations had there ever been a single reference to my "Southern type accent."

Showing my irritation would have been counterproductive, so I asked, "What can we do to deal with the situation?"

Howard had a solution.

"I'll hire a speech coach at company expense to work with you," he said. "And I'll let the key officers know what I've done, and will advise them of the results following your training."

I considered that a generous offer and readily accepted it.

The Human Resources Department provided me with the names of several highly recommended speech coaches. I selected one whose office in downtown San Francisco was near PG&E headquarters. We agreed to meet once a week for six weeks and then assess my progress.

The speech coach began by asking me whether I had any recordings of myself speaking formally. I provided her with several audio and video recordings of speeches, which she said she would review before we met the next time.

The first thing she said to me at that second meeting was puzzling.

"Why, again, are you here?"

I had no clue why she was asking me that, so I didn't

answer right away.

"I reviewed your speeches and listened very closely," she said. "You are a very persuasive speaker."

I explained that my diction and accent were concerns that might prevent me from moving forward and becoming an officer in the company.

"I'll work with you for the next few weeks," she said, "to see what improvements can be made."

She had video equipment right there in her office, and recorded interviews with me on several occasions. In addition, she also gave me assignments to make additional tape recordings at home. In the end, she did give me some useful pointers and drills to practice certain pronunciations. For example, when I pronounced the word *fire*, I left off the final *r*. And I did the same thing with *hire*. For four weeks, she gave me other minor but useful tips.

Finally, she said to me one day, "I'm taking PG&E's money for nothing. In my professional opinion, I haven't observed anything that genuinely warrants my continued services."

For our last two sessions, we listened to my speeches, and she gave me some really valuable feedback, but it had nothing to do with my diction. Most of all, she recommended that I tone down the intensity of my speaking style. Knowing my background as the son of a preacher, she pointed out that I sometimes sounded like one myself. That was learned behavior, which I had adopted over many years of exposure to the church. She helped me to lessen that intensity so as not to intimidate a corporate audience or appear to be preaching to them, which might be construed negatively.

Another good piece of advice that she gave me was to

"take the temperature" of the room or corporate setting before speaking. In other words, know the demographics of your audience, and adapt your language, style, and tone accordingly.

In the end, I was thankful to Howard for helping me to play the game well. Looking back on this obstacle, or potential obstacle, I learned that on my corporate journey, hurdles were going to be placed in front of me—at times designed to "bait" me to react inappropriately. Had I responded with anger, or had I sought to defend myself by citing my victory at the Supreme Court, I would have been labeled "arrogant" and criticized for lacking awareness of the finesse required of company officers. Instead, Howard and a speech coach protected me from all that.

With that problem out of the way, it was time to move up.

In late 1987, some fifteen years after I had first set foot in PG&E's headquarters on Beale Street, I made my first visit to the top, the thirty-second floor. Prior to that day, any meetings that I had attended with executives had been held in the conference rooms or offices of the legal department, one floor below. Perhaps other attorneys had visited the Executive Floor, but not I. The reason for my visit on this occasion was an appointment I had with Ellis Langley, the senior vice president who was the head of division operations, a meeting that had been arranged by my mentor, Dick Clarke.

It was Dick's theory that by my becoming a division manager, I would receive the practical knowledge about operations that would enhance my eligibility for promotion to vice president. That was certainly a career challenge, for the compensation a vice president was paid was more than what I was earning, and there weren't any Black officers at PG&E at the time. (Owen Davis, the first and only Black officer in that era, had died in October 1987.)

So, I went along with Dick's plan, although I knew that no other lawyer at PG&E who had been made an officer had been required to get operating experience as a division manager first. Since my legal ranking was above that of a division manager, I would have to move down to move up, but I was assured that I would keep my lawyer's salary.

The sit-down with the head of division operations turned out to be one of the strangest and most hilarious meetings in my career at PG&E. I really didn't know what to expect, but I was not anticipating an encounter with military brass. It turned out to be just that, but without the bugles blaring. The head of division operations was a former Colonel in the Army by the name of Ellis Langley, who looked like he had been sent over from the casting department of a Hollywood studio with a neatly styled crew cut, a cigar crunched between his teeth, and an intentionally intimidating manner. When his secretary announced that I had arrived, Colonel Langley invited me into his office and immediately spoke to me as if I were a questionable new recruit for a dangerous military mission.

"What's this I hear about you wanting to be a division manager?" he growled. "You're a lawyer. You don't know anything about operations. What do you know about gas and electricity? What do you know about running a division?"

Langley castigated me for at least twenty minutes for having the temerity to even come to talk to him about the possibility of being a division manager, and I had to take it. Although I felt slapped down, I must say that his behavior did not achieve its intended effect. Instead, it motivated me even more to want the job and to do it well.

(Many years later, when I ran into the Colonel at an event, long after I had succeeded in operations, he told me that he had been wrong about me. "You turned out to be a hell of a division manager!" he said.)

Not long after that interview, PG&E sent me to participate in the three-month-long Advanced Management Program (AMP) at Harvard Business School, to take courses in leadership, marketing, accounting, business relations, and more. That program was no picnic. First of all, I had to leave Glenda and my baby daughter, Brittany, behind. That was emotionally difficult, but Glenda was fully supportive, so, without hesitation, I moved to the campus of HBS in Boston, Massachusetts, to put in twelve-hour days, six days a week.

HBS's Advanced Management Program is considered one of the premier executive training programs for business executives around the world. At the end of the twelve-week program, HBS grants alumni status to its graduates. My class had 165 members, of whom four were Black and two were women. The curriculum, which was taught by nationally renowned professors, was rigorous, commencing daily at 8:00 A.M. and ending at 3:00 P.M., with lots of homework assignments. As in law school, the professors used the Socratic method to cross-examine the students, which ensured lively debate and discussion.

Also to encourage robust dialogue, the school divided the participants into small groups of ten, who not only studied together, but were expected to dine together off campus every Saturday evening. Each student was required to host a dinner at a place of his or her own choosing, which added more expense to the already outrageous cost of the program, $25,000. Fortunately, PG&E was picking up the tab.

For me, the most exciting courses were the ones on leadership, because that skill can be utilized in many different situations. Much of what I had learned as president of the National Bar Association and as Western Province Polemarch of Kappa Alpha Psi was validated by those courses.

In early October 1988, about halfway through the program, I received a call from Howard Golub, PG&E's general counsel. When I heard his voice, I was quite surprised, and I was even more surprised when he asked me to return to San Francisco for a special celebration. He then informed me that I was being promoted to level 15, the highest level in the legal department, just below himself.

At Harvard Business School

The celebration was set for the only weekend break the HBS program provided us. Returning home gave me an opportunity not only to celebrate my promotion, but, most importantly, to see Glenda and Brittany, who was 2 at the time.

I was especially appreciative of Glenda's tremendous support and sacrifice, which were helping to advance my career. While I was at HBS, Glenda was not only totally responsible for Brittany's care, but also had to maintain her medical practice.

When I returned to school that Sunday evening, I felt comfortable with my career decision and pursued my studies with even more zeal than before. A few weeks later, Glenda and Brittany came to Boston, as did many other families, to attend the ceremony that acknowledged the completion of AMP103. After that, we returned to the Bay Area, where I excitedly awaited my new career as a division manager.

My initial meeting for that position was scheduled for January 2, 1989. Bunnie Brown, my Black colleague in Human Resources, with whom I had regularly met for lunch since my early days at the company, who was intent on seeing Blacks rise to officer positions, prepped me for the interview with George Clifton, a regional vice president, by asking me standard questions I would be expected to answer, and critiquing me when I fell short.

As it turned out, my appointment to the position appeared to be a foregone conclusion. Even before the interview, it was clear to me that Clifton, to whom I would be reporting, had been given the opportunity—as a courtesy—to interview me, but not the power to reject me.

Bunnie had told me that I would probably be appointed to head a small division, such as the one in Napa County, forty miles north of San Francisco, where I could grow slowly. But that did not prove to be the case. Instead, I was selected to serve as division manager for the East Bay, known as the Central Division, one of PG&E's largest divisions, with 500 employees, an annual budget of $60 million, and annual revenues of several hundred million dollars. If that weren't daunting enough, there had been four division managers of the Central Division in the four previous years, and each one of them had only lasted a year at most. Obviously, the Central Division was one of the most challenging units in the company.

The outgoing division manager had had considerable difficulty managing the division, especially its Black employees, many of whom had complained about his unfair treatment of them. Of all the Blacks who worked in divisions at PG&E, roughly 70 percent worked in the East Bay, a region that includes Oakland. Because the former manager was very close to the regional vice president, he wasn't fired. Instead, he was transferred to run another division, a move that was touted as a promotion. I heard, however, that he didn't see it that way and was rather displeased with his reassignment. All I can say is that I thought it appropriate to attend his going-away party as a sign of good will. To signal a smooth transition, it would have been customary for him to introduce me at the party as his successor. But that didn't happen. Instead, he saw to it that I would be on my own.

23

Rookie in Charge

Deal with yourself as an individual, worthy of respect, and make everyone else deal with you the same way.

—Nikki Giovanni

I never lacked confidence, but that isn't to say that I blinded myself to some rather steep challenges I have faced at times in my career. Here was my first opportunity to run a major division of the company—or *any* division, for that matter. In fact, this was my first opportunity to supervise a large number of people, so I was clearly out of my comfort zone and uncertain exactly what to do.

Despite that, I went to work at 1919 Webster Street in Oakland, confident that if I could lead a volunteer organization such as Kappa Alpha Psi or the NBA, in which I had no power to fire anybody, then leading an organization in which I did have such power should not be really difficult. However, my intention was not to fire anyone in order to put in my own loyalists. Rather, I fully intended to work with the people I had, knowing that the essence of leadership is to inspire one's subordinates to be the best they can.

One absolutely fantastic person I inherited from my predecessors was the division secretary, Alline Adams. It is really difficult to describe the divine gift to me that Alline was. She had been born in Texas and had a really lovely accent and polite disposition that caused everyone who knew her to love her instantly. Furthermore, having a "sister," a Black angel, as my assistant was something I had not expected, and that was going to be a huge bonus.

My first order of business was to become acquainted with the department heads who would be reporting to me: the managers of gas and electric operations, public affairs, the Alameda office, human resources (HR), support services, customer services, and marketing.

Before I met any of those managers, however, the HR manager, Patricia (Pat) Shelton, came to me to make it clear that she knew I was inexperienced, but she wanted very much to help make me successful, especially since none of my four predecessors had lasted very long. I was appreciative of Pat's eagerness, so I invited her to join me on my first visit with the workers at Oakport, the service center for field employees. They were mostly union members, who took great pride in their jobs and were generally a cohesive group who enjoyed their work and were outstanding at doing it.

In the "Bull Room" at Oakport, where the crews gathered each morning before they left for their assignments, I was impressed to see several hundred men and women, the backbone of the operations of the Central Division, when I walked in. After Jim Dunnaway, the manager of gas and electric operations, introduced me, I spoke to the group forcefully about what I hoped to accomplish. For the most part, I was talking theory straight from my Harvard training, having forgotten the advice of my speech coach to first take the temperature of the room. I set forth a number of lofty ideas that I thought would be good business strategies. My audience listened attentively, and when I finished, I even received some polite applause.

After mingling with the group, shaking hands, and trying to begin learning names, I returned to my office in downtown Oakland, believing I had done a great job relating to the employees. Being a division manager, I thought, was going to be fun. A few minutes after I reached my desk, however, Pat came to my door with a grim look on her face.

"How did I do?" I said, beaming.

"Bob, you were lousy!" she replied with a smile. "The employees didn't understand a word you said. You totally failed to communicate with them."

That was a stunning dose of reality. When I asked Pat to elaborate, she spent the next half-hour explaining with examples why I had not connected with the employees. After I learned my lesson, we developed a plan to help me to communicate more effectively with the rank and file. Pat often accompanied me when I spoke to various groups of employees, watching closely from the sidelines. Whenever I failed to connect, she would take me aside, and then, waving her index finger like a disappointed teacher, she would say, "Bahhhd!"

Pat became my most trusted manager, my "White angel." I really needed her because George Clifton, my boss, was clearly not interested in mentoring me. He hadn't selected me, and I had replaced his friend, so he laid out specific goals for the division and made it clear that he didn't want to hear any excuses about my being new on the job. I had one year to turn things around.

With that objective, I set expectations for all my managers, knowing that I would only succeed if they were successful in their respective areas of responsibility. Clearly, I didn't have the technical knowledge or experience to tell them how to do their jobs, so I decided that the most important thing I could do was to provide the leadership to inspire them to want to be outstanding managers.

The toughest part of the division to manage was gas and electric operations, which was directly responsible for keeping the gas flowing and the lights burning. Furthermore, approximately 350 of the 500 people in my division worked in that department. Thus, my first focus was to review performance expectations with the manager, Jim Dunnaway, and encourage him to ensure that his department met its targets. Jim was a very likeable person, who was respected by his workers and also by those in other divisions.

At our first monthly meeting, Jim and I spent considerable time going over how I would assess his performance. I was especially interested in finding new ways to be more efficient in delivering gas and electric service to the customers. I made it clear—and Jim already knew—that I didn't have the technical ability to run his operations, but I was definitely going to hold him accountable for achieving expected results. I told him that he would be completely empowered to be innovative, so long as he kept me informed of what he was doing. Jim was very happy about that arrangement. At each stage of my dealings with him, I was careful to keep Pat fully engaged in the process, in order to make certain that I was not doing anything stupid.

By the end of my first month, all of my managers had performance targets set for their areas, and thereafter we met monthly as a group to monitor our performance as a division. We also instituted a number of team-building initiatives. In time, with the team feeling fully engaged, an air of achievement began to circulate throughout the Central Division. By June, six months into my job, we could all see definite improvements over the previous year's performance.

In the meantime, I was meeting each month with George Clifton to explain what was happening in the division. But try as I might to demonstrate my competence to him, I was aware through the grapevine that he was surreptitiously checking with some of my managers about my performance, which made me feel that I had little support from above. That made me worry that my performance would not be adequately reported if there were no one to sing my praises, which could block my plan to become a vice president.

When I spoke to Bunnie about the problem, she reasoned that so long as I did a good job running the division, the objective results would be visible to everyone. Still, I was concerned.

As part of building the spirit of our Central Division team, several members thought it would be a good idea to get together informally away from the workplace. So, on August 13, 1989, forty or fifty of us met at my home in the Oakland hills. Glenda, who very much wanted to be a part of the occasion, was eight months pregnant at the time. In fact, her water broke on that very morning, which meant that the baby might arrive at any moment. Therefore, rather than participate actively, Glenda decided to stay in her bed. But everyone else had a great time—and the very next day, our son, Phillip, was born.

That year, 1989, was turning out to be a momentous one, and it wasn't over yet. October brought us the Bay Area Baseball World Series. The first game was played on Tuesday evening, October 17, at Candlestick Park between the San Francisco Giants and the Oakland Athletics. At 5:04 P.M., Northern California residents and a national television audience of millions witnessed the Loma Prieta earthquake with a magnitude of 6.9. Sixty-three people lost their lives that day, over 3,700 others were injured, and damage amounted to nearly $6 billion.

I was in my office at 1919 Webster Street, talking on the phone with the customer services supervisor, when the building began to rock and roll from side to side. Then it shook intensely.

Recognizing that this was a "big one," I immediately ducked under my desk, as we had been trained to do, and for as long as twenty seconds, it felt like the world was spinning out of control. When the shaking settled down, I left my office to join others in the building to assess the damage, which we discovered was considerable. Nevertheless, for the most part, the building appeared to be safe.

By now, news was beginning to come in that a double-decker section of Interstate 880 in West Oakland had collapsed, trapping numerous commuters, and perhaps killing many of them. Electric power had been knocked out in many parts of the Central Division, and there were gas outages and eruptions everywhere.

I immediately called Jim, my gas and electric operations

manager, who told me that his crews were assembling as we spoke, preparing to hit the road to restore service wherever it had been disrupted. I headed to Oakport to be at his side as the crews deployed. They were awesome, working night and day to restore service as quickly as possible. I was proud of those crews in the Central Division.

After Throwing the First Pitch at an A's Game

A month later, I would be receiving feedback about my first year as Central division manager, and I didn't have a good feeling about that because I sensed George Clifton did not really believe an attorney was best suited to leading an operations unit. In fact, he only rated my performance as "acceptable." The division's performance had improved in every category over the previous year, which was great news, but George noted that although the division had done well in the aftermath of the earthquake and had improved its overall performance, that was due to the excellent performance of my managers.

I found that evaluation incredible! Had the division's performance fallen below that of the previous year, I would have been blamed for the poor showing. Furthermore, if its performance in the aftermath of the earthquake had been disappointing, the blame would have been mine, too. The fact that I received no credit confirmed my worst fears: George was not my advocate, to say the least. I had no choice but to continue to try to prove myself, with my eyes on the prize.

In one's personal life and career, one has to know which battles to fight and which ones to ignore. Some people fight for the sake of fighting, which is unfortunate and self-destructive. When you don't know how to pick your battles, you might find yourself in a constant state of war on all fronts. So, choosing battles you can win is your first challenge. But equally critical is determining ahead of engagement whether the battle is worth it. Sometimes it's best to simply swallow your pride and move on.

I had been a division manager for a year and a half when a potential battle was suddenly thrust upon me. It came early one morning, shortly after I arrived for work. From the very beginning, I had established a routine of arriving before dawn to get my paperwork and other things done, so I could spend more time out in the field with the crews, getting to know all the supervisors and many of the employees in my division. Around 5:30 or 6:00 A.M., I received an unexpected phone call from the man I had replaced as division manager.

As I pointed out earlier, he was disgruntled, and I had been made aware that he was regularly taking potshots at the Central Division, and at me in particular. I had ignored those slights, expecting them to eventually end, but as our division became a top performer, he became more and more resentful. When the phone rang that morning, I didn't know who was calling. I simply answered and identified myself.

The caller did not identify himself, but I immediately recognized his voice as he let out every bad feeling he had been holding onto about me for the past eighteen months. He accused me of undermining him by maneuvering to get him transferred to another division, so I could take his place. In fact, I didn't know him at all at the time, or that he had been the division manager. The man was ranting and raving, screaming so loud that I had to hold the phone away from my ear and fight the urge to laugh. This went on for a good ten minutes. Then it occurred to me that if he were carrying on to such a degree at this hour of the morning, he had probably lost his ability to think rationally.

Recognizing this, I stopped myself from getting upset at the insults pounding in my ear, because the situation was no longer laughable. When he finally calmed down a bit, I said, "Thank you for calling. I understand how you're feeling. You should think about what you've said. After you reflect for a while, you might feel differently."

I could have tried to defend myself. I could have responded to every accusation he made, some of which were quite piercing. I could have reported him to upper management. But I knew that this was not a battle I wanted to fight, for I had nothing to gain from winning it. That simply would have dragged me into another battle. What he had to say to me privately on the phone before dawn really had no impact either on my progress or my reputation, so why lose my temper? Moreover, to whom would I complain? Our common boss, George Clifton, was *his* friend, not mine. Later that day, at a company meeting, I saw my predecessor, who appeared to be in a totally different mood. Now he was quite rational, and never once mentioned our conversation. Nor did I. In fact, I never had an issue or an encounter with him again.

Congratulating Employees

When I had been a division manager for about two years, I received a call one morning from one of my Black colleagues, Roberta Bradley, who informed me that there was a campaign of negative comments circulating about me among the officer ranks. The comments, Roberta said, had been part of the official discussion at one of the officers' meetings, in which there was talk of whether or not my name should be placed on the list of candidates who might become future officers of the company. Given my ambitions, the damaging remarks needed to be addressed.

Earlier, the obstacle raised to my becoming an officer was my Southern diction and accent. This new obstacle was called the "Bob Harris Love Me Wall."

The year when this was brought to my attention was 1991. At that point, I had been active for twenty years or more in the Kappas, the Charles Houston Bar Association, the National Bar Association, the NAACP, and other organizations that served the Black community. Therefore, I had a wall in my office that was covered with awards that recognized my service and leadership. I associated those with memories of years spent with colleagues and friends on meaningful projects. They were never about personal glory, and it had never occurred to me that some people might find those awards intimidating enough to disparage my character in order to discount my achievements within the company. What treachery!

The wall in question was not some kind of throne. It wasn't behind my desk, but rather faced me. Visitors sat with their backs to it, and would only get a glimpse of it when they left the office. My assistant, Alline, frequently allowed employees to visit my office when I wasn't there—especially Black employees, who had never before had the opportunity to visit the office of a Black division manager. Alline told me that those visitors sometimes commented that the wall was a source of great pride to them.

Now comments were circulating, especially among the officers, that I had placed those awards on my wall to boost my own ego and let others know of my "superiority." Roberta Bradley said she had heard from a reliable source, a participant in an officers' meeting, that a discussion about succession planning and who might rise to the level of officer had ended up becoming a discussion about the "Bob Harris Love Me Wall." Rather than focusing on my capabilities as a division manager, the officers had spent their time talking about the awards on my wall.

I was more than a bit upset that something so trivial could potentially derail my upward mobility in the company. As when an issue had been made of my diction, I felt that an obstacle was being raised that had nothing to do with my performance and nothing to do with my capability to serve the company effectively as an officer. This was clearly a moment of reckoning. How I chose to respond would decide whether I was still in the game. The issue may have been small, but if I defended myself, my words might be misconstrued and used against me as proof that I was "full of myself." Was I being baited to confirm the suspicion that I was not officer material?

When I got off the phone, I attempted to consider objectively how some people might perceive a wall of awards in anyone's office—and, in particular, the office of a Black man. Over the next several days, I sought the advice of my colleagues within PG&E, especially my Black colleagues, and friends and allies outside the company, my typical procedure before making sensitive critical decisions. Whether the issue of the wall were real or imagined, I realized that if I did nothing, I would invite a repeat of the officers' discussion about me at a future meeting related to promotion to their ranks. I had to get them off the topic of the "Love Me Wall."

The first thing I did was ask Alline to arrange for the building department to take down most of the plaques, leaving only the ones framing my college degree, my law degree, and my admission to the bar. That ended the discussion of the "Love Me Wall."

That incident was another learning opportunity for me. In the corporate setting, an obstacle can appear that has nothing to do with performance, but is nonetheless capable of deciding the direction of one's career. Relationships and perceptions are nearly as important as performance. The officers in the meeting where talk of the wall had come up were all White. Luckily, Roberta Bradley had a close friendship with one of them, who shared the intelligence with her. If I had not been good friends with her, she might not have passed it on to me. You never know where valuable information and assistance will come from.

I served as manager of the Central Division from January 1989 to March 1993. The biggest challenge I faced during my tenure in the division was the Oakland firestorm, which killed twenty-five people, injured 150 others, wiped out over 2,800 single-family homes, and obliterated more than 400 apartment and condominium units in one day, a Sunday, October 20, 1991. The eyes of the nation were focused on Oakland's response to the tragedy, the largest and most devastating urban fire in the history of the country.

The firestorm originated from a small grass fire near Highway 24 on the Berkeley-Oakland border. It had not been completely put out, and when strong winds picked up, the next morning, the flames were reignited and spread rapidly. I knew nothing about it, since I was on an airliner headed back to the Bay Area from a weekend meeting in New York of the National Bar Association. When my flight landed in San Francisco around 1:30 P.M., I headed for my parked car, eager to get home to my wife and two small children.

As I pulled out of the lot, I saw a dark cloud across the bay in the Oakland area. Curious, I turned on my radio and learned that there was a major fire sweeping through the Oakland hills, which had been raging out of control since 11:00 that morning. I immediately knew that meant trouble for my division, so I wanted assurance that we were prepared to respond. Reaching for my car cellphone, I tried to call Oakport, the service yard where the crews would have assembled, but there was no answer. As I arrived at my office on Webster Street, I noticed that ash and other residue from the firestorm were drifting down onto the parking lot. Fortunately, when I phoned Oakport again, this time I was able to reach Jim.

"Bob, this is *really* bad," he said. "But our electric and gas crews are out there, prepared to shut off gas mains and valves as well to ensure that downed electric wires do not pose a danger to the public."

I thanked him for being on the job and told him I would join him at Oakport after I stopped by my home. I soon learned that the firestorm was in the Montclair and Rockridge areas, about five miles from my house, so Glenda and the kids were safe.

When I arrived at Oakport, someone in the yard told me that Jim was on the roof of the building, observing what he could see of the raging fire. When I got up there, I joined him and George Clifton, my boss, in watching enormous clouds of black smoke billowing over the hills. After fifteen minutes, we went down to Jim's office to map out a strategy for restoring utility service once the fire was declared under control. After looking at all aspects of the restoration process to ensure that we had adequate materials to make repairs, it was obvious that we couldn't handle this disaster alone. So, we placed crews in every operations division as far away as Bakersfield on notice to be prepared to assist in the restoration.

Around 7:00 P.M., we decided to take a tour of the area around the Claremont Hotel to get a feel for the enormity of the disaster facing us. All the streets were blocked off by the Oakland police and fire departments, but since we were PG&E officials, we were allowed into the area, with the warning that we were surrounded by fires. At one point, just as we got out of our vehicle, a shooting ball of fire hit a pine tree just a few feet away from us, setting it ablaze.

That was it! I told Jim it was time to get out of there, which we promptly did. As we returned to Oakport, with everything burning, we knew that there was nothing else we could do that evening, and it was best to get prepared for the next day, when hopefully the fire would have died down.

When I awoke at 5:00 A.M. on Monday, I learned that the winds had calmed considerably, and a major portion of the firestorm was under control, although small fires were still burning in some places. Skipping breakfast, I headed down to 1919 Webster for a meeting with my customer services manager, whom I had telephoned the night before, asking him to meet me and present his plans for dealing with the crisis. Before I could reach the office, however, he called me, sounding frantic.

"Bob," he said, "I've got to see you right away!"

When I arrived, I immediately headed to his office.

"This is too much for me, Bob," he said, looking disheveled. "I was up most of the night and couldn't get my head around what we need to do. I'm resigning!"

In the middle of a major crisis, I was losing a key manager! *What the hell is going on?* I thought.

Without showing any emotion, I simply said, "I'll find a way to deal with the situation."

As I rushed to my office, I remembered a recent visit to another division, where I had met a woman named Michelle Silva, who had struck me as an outstanding customer services manager.

"I need your help right away," I pleaded over the phone.

By 9:00 A.M., she was in the customer service office, making plans to deal with the problems we were starting to have with customers who were asking when they would get their service back.

A big problem for us was that while the fire had consumed whole blocks of homes, it had somehow eerily skipped over others, leaving a number of houses intact. The question was: Given that many gas and electrical facilities had been disabled, how would service be restored to the surviving homes in a timely manner?

The initial prediction by our corporate experts around 10:00 A.M. was that it would probably take at least two weeks before service could be fully restored. That seemed like a long time to me, but I was a lawyer who had been a division manager for less than three years and who had never dealt with this magnitude of destruction, so who was *I* to question that estimate?

Around 2:00 o'clock, Dick Clarke, the CEO of PG&E, and my mentor, along with Grant Horne, the vice president of corporate communications, toured the fire area with me and also visited the crews at Oakport. Both of them told me that all media contacts would be through me as Central Division manager, rather than through corporate headquarters in San Francisco. Having had media training and numerous media experiences internally and externally, I had no fears about being the company spokesman and saying what was appropriate.

At one point, however, when Grant and I were chatting, he cautioned me not to make any promises for restoration of service other than to follow the company line that it would likely be two weeks before service was restored.

A little later, when Dick and I were alone for a moment, he said, as he gave me a pat on the back, "Your leadership, Bob, clearly indicates that you should be an officer, and I can assure you that is going to happen."

However, he didn't say when, and I didn't ask, given that I was fully focused on handling the crisis we were facing. I did recognize, though, that I was being watched closely, and any misstep would be a strike against me.

Later that afternoon, I consulted with my team, who, after assessing the situation for a while, concluded that we could restore service within days, not weeks. By Friday, October 25th, they said, everything would be up and running. Five days!

After hearing from my confident team that service would be restored by Friday, I reflected on my commitment to Grant to stay with the two-week estimate. As I headed home, I hoped this would not become an issue.

Daily news conferences were scheduled to begin the next day, to update the media and the public on our progress. So, early on Tuesday morning, as I was preparing to leave for Oakport, I received a call from a reporter at KRON-TV, who wanted to talk about PG&E's efforts to restore service.

"How long will it take?" he asked.

"I'm not sure," I said.

When I got to Oakport, after reviewing with my team the progress we had already made in restoring service, I asked them to reconsider their Friday estimate. Without any dissent, they all remained steadfast.

At the 1:00 P.M. news briefing, after I gave details of damage and other issues related to the firestorm, the "when" question was one of the first to be asked. I paused for a moment and then looked directly at the camera.

"For those whose homes are capable of receiving gas and electric service," I said, "their service will be restored by five P.M. Friday."

Almost immediately, that announcement was broadcast with headlines like "PG&E Says Power Back on by Friday!"

It didn't take long for my pager to start buzzing. It was Grant, demanding to talk to me. Obviously, I knew why he was calling, so I quickly returned his call.

"Bob!" he began. "Why did you make that ridiculous promise of restoring service by Friday?"

I hesitated for a couple of seconds before responding, "I made that statement because my people promised me they would have power back by Friday."

"And you *believed* them?" he said, sounding angry and incredulous.

"Yes, of course, I believed them."

"Then, you're crazy! This is an example of making a promise that you can't fulfill. You should know that this will reflect unfavorably on you as a manager, and will seriously harm the company's reputation when service is *not* restored by Friday."

But his threats didn't bother me, because I had faith in my team. When I told them what Grant had said, they became even more determined.

Late on Friday afternoon, it began to rain, which added to the suspense. But around 4:00 P.M., corporate communications, Grant's department, issued a news bulletin, announcing that PG&E had restored service to all the homes in the firestorm area that were capable of receiving it.

In a time of crisis, the company instantly became a hero. The *Oakland Tribune* gave all the other services and organizations, from the police department to the water company, an *A* for their efforts. But they gave PG&E an *A+*. Even Grant called to congratulate me and all the employees on a job well done.

Looking back, I can see Grant's prudence in directing me not to promise more than I could deliver. In repairs, you never know what problems crews may encounter and be stymied by. Clearly, I had taken a risk when I had unswerving faith in my team, and was also motivated by how difficult a time it was for thousands of people whose lives had been disrupted by the firestorm. Two of them, incidentally—my daughter's godparents, James and Ada Cole—were temporarily staying in my home, having been displaced from their own in Montclair.

24

Broken Promises

Power concedes nothing without a demand. It never did and it never will. Find out just what any people will quietly submit to, and you have found out the exact measure of injustice and wrong which will be imposed upon them, and these will continue till they are resisted with either words or blows, or with both.

—Frederick Douglass

After four successful years in Oakland, during which I improved the Central Division's reputation from one of the lowest-performing divisions to one of the highest, I was itching to move up. My eyes had long been set on rising to the Executive Floor, a promotion that Dick Clarke had promised me when I agreed to become a division manager.

Remember, Oakland had been presented to me as a necessary stepping stone, and I had made the leap, although I knew of no White lawyers, including Dick, who had been forced to get operations experience before being considered for an executive position. The one Black officer in PG&E, Owen Davis, who had succumbed to pancreatic cancer four years earlier, in 1987, had been a nuclear engineer and a division manager before his promotion to vice president.

My first real shot at the Executive Floor came in the late spring of 1993, when word spread that PG&E's board of directors would be meeting to choose some new vice presidents. Naturally, I anticipated that my name would be on the list. Then a rumor started on a Monday that there would be a vote that Friday, with an announcement the following week. The tension for me during those seven days was intense— almost as extreme as the pressure I had felt during the week before the bar exam results came in the mail. In both cases, I had worked very hard to achieve a favorable outcome. But, as everyone knows, success is never guaranteed.

At first, I was reasonably optimistic, but as the week progressed, I had a gnawing feeling that something was awry, and it wasn't mere intuition. I knew that if any managers were going to be made officers, the CEO or someone else high up in the company would have spoken with them ahead of any announcement. In other words, the candidates would be told informally in order to obtain their consent. That's just standard operating procedure—and *I* hadn't gotten that call.

On the Saturday afternoon before the announcement, however, I did receive a call at home from Dick Clarke. After a brief exchange of light conversation, we got down to the point. The man who had been my mentor from Day One, helping me to cultivate my career over twenty years, let me know that on Monday, as rumored, several new vice presidents would be announced. But I would not be among them.

"Several officers," he said, "are adamantly opposed to you being named a vice president. I fought vigorously for your appointment, but in the end, tough as it was for me, I relented. So, you have two options. You can remain Central Division manager, in which case you should call Virgil Rose, or you can return to the legal department, in which case you should call Howard Golub."

At that moment, I didn't know exactly which way to go, but I did have one stipulation if I were to choose to return to the legal department. The only thing I could think of in that deflating moment was to fight for more money. I let Dick know that if I had stayed in the legal department and not left for the operational experience, I would by now have received certain increases in salary. Instead, my salary had been stagnant for four years because, when I took the Oakland job, I was already making more than division managers were paid. If I chose to return to the legal department, I wanted my compensation to reflect what it would have been with normal raises had I never left. Dick agreed.

When I told Glenda about what was one of the most disillusioning moments in my entire career, I was nearly knocked out, but she was outraged.

"Those no good double crossers!" she said. "You should sue them for what they've done to you! You should have listened to me. I never trusted them in the first place."

The board's decision upended my expectations for my whole career path. And with Dick not standing up for me, I wondered if he had deceived me by putting me on a bridge to nowhere when he had encouraged me to get operations experience, with the promise that I would become an officer. I certainly felt deserted.

Glenda and I spent time, painfully replaying my career

choices. Where had I gone wrong? Had I misplaced my trust in Dick? I even considered leaving PG&E. For someone with my qualifications, surely there would be several exciting opportunities elsewhere. I was at a crossroads, having done everything that I had been asked to do. I was down, troubled, and confused, but I wasn't ready to give up. Glenda, on the other hand, was mad as hell.

Later that Saturday afternoon, I telephoned Virgil Rose, the senior vice president of divisions, to tell him about my conversation with Dick. To test the waters, I wanted to find out if he really wanted me to stay in Oakland. I needed to get a feel for his position, and he certainly gave it to me. With a polite but chilly reception, he made me understand that he would accept any decision I made, but I didn't have his full support to remain as a division manager. I think that, like George Clifton, Virgil's assessment of me was influenced by the fact that I had come to the Central Division from the legal department and not up through the ranks. I had never had a bad experience with Virgil. Nevertheless, since he was the senior officer of the region in which I was a division manager, his recommendation for my promotion would probably have been decisive. By the same token, his objection to my promotion would have been decisive. Our conversation, which was short, ended without me making a commitment one way or the other. It was clear to me, though, that he had not been supportive of my entrance into the officer ranks in the first place.

My next call was to Howard Golub, PG&E's general counsel, whose reaction immediately told me what I needed to hear.

"Bob," he said, "I really want you back in the legal

department. You're an outstanding lawyer, with much to offer PG&E, and I'm anxious for you to rejoin us."

Howard had been my supporter for a long time. He had come into the legal department at about the same time as I had, but he was ahead of me, since he had already practiced law for a number of years in the Navy. We had immediately hit it off as friends, and I was one of the few attorneys in the company that he seemed to respect. He didn't speak to me as a superior, but rather as the old friend that he was. His tone was comforting as he laid out an acceptable plan for my return to a position of responsibility.

"I'll make certain," he said, "that you're well received. On Monday morning, I'll send out a memo indicating that you're returning to the law department."

With Glenda

So, we decided in the course of that conversation that I would be returning to the thirty-first floor on Beale Street—which I did a week later, as soon as I closed out my responsibilities in the Central Division.

Before I set foot back in corporate headquarters, I had

decided to approach the situation with a positive attitude. I was determined to do my best in the legal department, working just as hard as I had before. Nevertheless, I was not giving up my dream to become a vice president of PG&E. My head was "bloody but unbowed." I strongly believed that I would find a way to achieve my goal, even though at the time I had no clear idea how I would do that.

Returning to the legal department after four years was not a bitter pill to swallow. I was determined that I wasn't going backward but forward. Although I felt that some of my colleagues saw me as a returning prodigal son, who had wasted his father's wealth, I persuaded myself that I had no reason to feel embarrassed or shamed. I had been a dutiful son by doing what senior management had asked of me.

Howard welcomed me back with as many riches and as much warmth as the father in the parable greeted his son. My salary as a division manager at the time was about $100,000. When I returned to the legal department, it went up by about $60,000.

The word that I had not been made a vice president spread quickly inside and outside the company. Without my knowledge, some influential friends made phone calls to Dick Clarke, asking why I hadn't been promoted. Those complaining calls came from a varied group of people, including Willie Brown, the Speaker of the California State Assembly; my longtime friend, Assemblywoman Gwen Moore, who was the chair of the Public Utilities Committee in the State Assembly; and my best friend, Elihu Harris, who was then Mayor of Oakland.

At some point, Elihu let me know that he had led a cadre of people, who had each argued to Dick Clarke that the failure to promote me could not have been based on performance, because I had excelled as both a lawyer and division manager. Therefore, it must have had to do with internal politics—or "something else."

I had no idea what would come of Elihu's pressure, but knowing him, I was certain he would never let go.

A few days later, Dick Clarke called to invite me to lunch. I knew that he was still my friend and still my mentor, so I suspected that he was feeling guilty about caving in on my promotion and perhaps wanted to give me a pep talk. When we met, he revealed to me that considerable pressure had been exerted by some of the senior officers to *not* make me a vice president. He then looked me squarely in the eyes.

"Bob," he said, "I was wrong. I shouldn't have listened to them. I'm going to make you a vice president. But we have to do it in the right way. Will you work with me to make it happen in the next six months or so?"

"Yes," I said. "Happy to."

Then he revealed his plan of action to me. I would become executive assistant to the president, Stan Skinner, for several months, after which Dick would announce that I was going to be appointed vice president of community and local governmental relations. Stan, who was a former member of the legal department, was on board with the plan.

Everything worked out perfectly. After I had served for five months as Stan's executive assistant, Dick announced that I had been elected a vice president of PG&E.

Setbacks, as I said earlier, are nothing more than setups for comebacks.

My tenure as vice president of community and local

governmental relations was both exciting and busy. I worked tirelessly to cement the corporation's good reputation within the various communities it served. We had a vision at PG&E to become a "neighbor of choice," meaning that we would demonstrate our commitment to the neighborhoods in which our plants and facilities were located by showing a concern for local causes.

One of the unique aspects of a public utility is its inability, unlike other companies, to move its physical assets elsewhere. Because of its infrastructure, a utility is tied to the communities in which it operates. Therefore, maintaining good relations is essential to its ability to operate effectively and efficiently.

As vice president of community and local governmental relations, I endeavored to bring life to the concept of being a neighbor of choice, and my team pursued that goal with passion, seizing every opportunity to be engaged.

PG&E's chief economist, Tapan Munroe, who reported directly to me, firmly believed that a strong corporate involvement enhanced economic vitality in the community. One day, Tapan came to me with a suggestion.

"Bob," he said, "I think PG&E can do more to help stimulate economic vitality here in the Bay Area. I've been looking at the work of Professor Michael Porter of the Harvard Business School, and I think his theory of competitive advantage can work here in this area."

"I'm familiar with his theory," I said. "And I know Professor Porter from my days at Harvard."

"Basically," Tapan said, "his idea is that inner cities can become more competitive economically by utilizing their populations as a source of talent and consumption."

A few weeks later, Tapan and I traveled to Boston to meet with Professor Porter, who subsequently came out to San Francisco to promote his theory—not only with PG&E, but with numerous leaders of other major corporations in the Bay Area, including Chevron, Bank of America, and Clorox.

Alline Adams, Ingrid Monroe, & Tapan Monroe

Adopting Professor Porter's model, PG&E funded the Oakland Communications Business Cluster Incubator and the Oakland Inner City Competitiveness Project, which today is known as the Inner City Advisors. A year later, Congressman Ronald V. Dellums of Oakland applauded PG&E in the Congressional Record for both projects.

"In the face of economic stagnation, military base closings, and downsizing throughout Northern California," Dellums said, "PG&E played a key role in bringing stakeholders together to forge a strategic plan for Oakland's future."

In addition, the Edison Electric Institute awarded PG&E one of its highest honors for its community engagement.

Then came trouble.

25

Rattlesnakes Never Sleep

There are times when life's ends are so raveled that reason and sense cry out that we stop and gather them together again before we can proceed.

—Richard Wright

The trouble began in early 1996 with an internal power skirmish in PG&E—a minor incident that led to a major effort to get rid of me.

The first confrontation was between one of my community relations managers, Tom Evans, who was responsible for San Francisco, and a senior vice president, Tom High, who was the assistant to the CEO, Stan Skinner.

Evans, who had earlier been a San Francisco division manager, had developed during that time an excellent relationship with one of the members of PG&E's board of directors. When a rather routine issue surfaced, the board member contacted Evans to resolve it, which he promptly did. Later, in a casual conversation with High, the board member allegedly told him how pleased she was with Evans's quick resolution of her issue. No big deal, right? Wrong!

High, who normally handled issues raised by board

members, considered this a serious breach of protocol. When he called Evans to read him the riot act, Evans—who reported to me—was quite upset. High, he said, was irrational and unusually harsh in criticizing him for what was really a trivial matter.

"No one has ever talked to me like that in my career," Evans said. He wanted to alert me that I would be hearing from High.

In fact, I received that call within an hour. High was clearly just as upset as Evans had described. After he vented his rage, I told him I already knew about the situation from Evans.

"What are you going to do about it?" he demanded to know.

"I'm not going to do anything about it," I said, "because you've already reprimanded Evans, and, in my opinion, overblown the situation. I think Evans has been punished more than enough for an insignificant matter. And, as far as I'm concerned, this is the end of the matter."

At that point, I was finished with High, but I suspected that High wasn't finished with me.

It didn't take long.

In the spring of 1996, the most contentious political issue in California was Proposition 209, an anti-affirmative-action ballot measure, which was heavily supported by the Republican Party and its leader, Governor Pete Wilson. Insidiously, though, the face of the proposition was a Black man, Ward Connerly, a member of the University of California Board of Regents, who had himself benefitted enormously from affirmative action programs.

Prop 209 was called the California Civil Rights Initiative. That, I believe, was also insidious, in that the title had been deliberately selected to deceive voters. For people who didn't keep up with the news, they might cast a yes vote, thinking they were supporting civil rights for minorities, when, in fact, just the opposite was true. The clear intent of Prop 209 was to prohibit colleges, universities, and government agencies from considering race as a factor in achieving diversity.

During the campaign, minority groups across the state, along with other organizations which supported programs that encouraged diversity, rallied against Prop 209. Missing from the debate was the voice of big corporations, many of whom in the mid-1990s were openly championing the benefits of a diverse workforce. The Greenlining Institute, an organization that worked to bring the American Dream within reach of everyone, regardless of race or income, was one of the many groups leading the opposition to Prop 209.

For several years, the institute had been engaged in a partnership with PG&E to work on issues of mutual concern. I had had a number of discussions about the lack of corporate opposition to Prop 209 with the institute's general counsel, Bob Gnaizda, who had been a friend of mine from our early days as lawyers, and with John Gamboa, the president of Greenlining. Both of them firmly believed that it was important for corporations to weigh in on the issue. We agreed that getting at least one corporation to take the lead in opposing Prop 209 would be a giant step. Since we all had a good relationship with Stan Skinner, we decided to talk with him about the issue.

I expected a fair response from Stan, who had a plaque hanging on his office wall that read: "YOU ONLY GET ONE CHANCE TO MAKE A GOOD FIRST IMPRESSION." When the three of us went together to see him, Stan was cautious. Prop 209, he said, was a "hot political issue, so considerably more thought has to be given to the backlash PG&E might face if we go on record in opposition. I'm sympathetic, but you should talk to Bob Glynn first."

At that time, Bob Glynn was the President of PG&E, who would succeed Stan as CEO in a few weeks. When we had that meeting with Bob, he was supportive, saying that he would take the matter under consideration. However, after a few weeks, there was still no response from him. Instead, he sent out a routine memorandum to all employees, touting the virtues of diversity and, most importantly, stating that diversity was a "core value" of the company.

Since the memorandum made no mention of Prop 209, I seized the moment by emailing Bob, who was now the CEO, to argue that if diversity were, indeed, a core value of the company, why were we remaining silent on an issue that was essential to that value, when we knew that Prop 209 was designed to eliminate diversity? I went on to remind him that it is easy to *talk* about diversity, but we were squarely facing an issue that put our core values to the test.

I thought that would provoke a response, and it did. Within a week, I learned that PG&E would publicly oppose the proposition. I immediately called Bob Gnaizda and John Gamboa to ask them not to tell anyone until PG&E figured out how best to make the announcement itself. Thrilled with the decision, they agreed to wait.

Tom High, however, was none too pleased, arguing that the decision would cause problems with the governor's office and with other supporters of Prop 209. He was acutely aware, of course, of my active role in pushing for the decision, and that compounded his problems with me, since he felt that I had unduly influenced Bob Glynn.

The immediate question was how and when to announce the company's opposition to the proposition. On both matters, Tom persuaded Bob not to make an announcement immediately, for fear of retaliation. Obviously, since time was of the essence, I was not pleased, but there was nothing I could do. So, for a couple of weeks, the announcement remained in limbo.

While I was attending a national convention of the NBA, I received a call from Alline Adams, my assistant, to let me know that Bob Glynn wanted to speak to me. When I called him, he told me that word had leaked out that PG&E was opposed to Prop 209, and therefore a press release was about to be issued confirming that news.

Once PG&E publicly announced its position, Governor Wilson was furious. He vented his anger to Stan Skinner, both in a phone call and a letter. Moreover, he contacted the heads of a number of other major corporations with the intention of discouraging them from joining PG&E.

Because of the fierce pressure exerted by the governor's office, PG&E decided not to make any financial contributions to the campaign to defeat Prop 209. This was clearly a compromise to placate Governor Wilson and supporters of the proposition, a decision that I think showed a lack of courage in the heat of battle.

Despite our best efforts, Prop 209 passed with 54 percent of the vote. Nevertheless, although we didn't save affirmative action, I believe that our stance was a clear success from a community relations and public affairs perspective. Across the state, PG&E received many accolades from opponents of Prop 209, especially from minority communities, and gained huge amounts of political and social capital for its stand. The company was even recognized by the U.S. Department of Labor, which bestowed its top honor on PG&E, the Opportunity 2000 Award. As I accepted that award on behalf of the company, Secretary of Labor Alexis Herman, referring to PG&E's opposition to Prop 209, stated: "Certainly, as they have demonstrated from their history, they have been willing to take tough stands on tough issues that have resulted in the real empowerment of their people."

Although the company received good publicity for its efforts, there were still rumblings of discontent on the Executive Floor. By June 1997, a complex and elaborate plot began to unfold. I had no idea when or how it developed, or exactly who was a part of the conspiracy, but after I returned from the annual NBA conference in August, I learned that a decision had been made to dismantle the Community and Local Governmental Relations Department.

The saga began on the Monday morning when I arrived for work, thinking everything was business as usual. The day started routinely with a staff meeting of the business unit officers, of which my department was a part. At the end of the meeting, my boss, Jim Randolph, senior vice president and general manager of the distribution and customer service business unit, without making eye contact, asked me to have lunch with him, something he had never done before.

At the restaurant, he began by rambling on in general terms about the business unit and the role of my department, which I found to be strange because there seemed to be no point he was trying to make. At the end of lunch, however, he said that some changes had occurred while I was out of town, and I needed to talk about them with Dan Richard, the senior vice president of governmental relations. Jim appeared to be distracted and was still evading eye contact. From that I knew something was going on, especially since he kept insisting that I needed to see Dan Richard.

Why can't you tell me? I wondered. *Why Dan, who works directly under Tom High?*

As I walked over to Dan's office, right after lunch, all kinds of thoughts were rushing through my mind.

Surely, I reasoned, *they wouldn't make any drastic changes without, at least, consulting me.*

After Dan and I exchanged niceties, I asked, "What's going on, Dan?"

We knew each other fairly well and had a cordial relationship, so he spoke frankly.

"We've decided," he said, "to abolish the Community and Local Governmental Relations Department."

"You must be joking," I said, literally unable to believe my ears.

"No," he said. "A determination has been made that PG&E doesn't need a Community and Local Governmental Relations Department anymore, because the company is so well respected in the communities it serves. The money allocated to operating your department could be better spent with Community Relations no longer under Jim Randolph's Business Unit, but instead a function of my Governmental Relations Unit."

"But," I said, bringing up the obvious, "PG&E's sterling

relationship in the communities it serves is due to the work of my department."

After a long pause, he said, "Bob, the decision has been made, so we'll work out the details later."

"What about the Local Governmental Relations part of my department?" I asked. "What happens to that?"

"That's already been shifted to Frank Regan's department," said.

Frank was the Vice President of State Governmental Relations, so local governmental relations were being merged with state governmental relation, which I had to admit had some rationale. But abolishing the community relations part of my department made no sense to me.

As I returned to my office, it was clear to me that Dan could not defend a decision that apparently had been made by someone else. But I never suspected that such a dramatic move would be made without at least some prior discussion with me. That's what knocked me off my feet. At that point, I knew I was being derailed and that a major assault was under way. Not prepared for the attack, I knew I had to play it cool rather than explode.

The first thing I suspected was that Tom High had found a way to strike back at me. Then it hit me like a bolt of lightning. Of course, he had! Dan and Tom were close allies. So, here it was. After that meeting with Dan, I assumed that the foundation had been laid by Tom not only to punish me but to ultimately provoke me into resigning from the company. Obviously, Dan had been commissioned to make that happen without disclosing Tom's role.

After trying to recuperate from the shock of what had just

happened, I realized that the ultimate goal was to humiliate me by making me an officer without portfolio. I had to admit that I had been outfoxed. This was serious business, and at the moment I was losing badly.

Lawyer that I am, I knew it was time to get more objective advice from my close legal friends, Elihu Harris and John Burris. After laying out the details to them, each one counseled me not to get emotional or do anything rash.

"As for now," John said, "you still have a job. Robert, that's a great position to be in. You get paid *not* to work while you figure out how to deal with them."

Elihu took the same position. "They'll be paying you to figure out how to kill them!" he said.

We had a good laugh at that, and I felt less frightened about being in the snake pit.

Later that night, I decided to send Dan an email, which stated, in part: "I appreciate the dialogue we had earlier today regarding the consolidation of the Community Relations and Governmental Relations Departments, which I learned about while I was out of state." I also told him that the change was "a complete surprise to me." Following up on his assertion that I would still be an "important" officer in the company, which I knew was a joke, I noted, "For me, it is important that I have a respected (both internally and externally) officer position, and not one merely with a title and ephemeral responsibilities. The worst possible situation mentally is to be in a situation where all your duties have been assigned to another person, leaving the impression for others that you are an officer without portfolio, since this would be a lose-lose proposition for all."

To make clear that I was a team player, I then wrote, "I

remain flexible regarding a new assignment, but I want it to be a truly meaningful one that's respected at PG&E and in the community."

After receipt of that email, Dan had to realize that I knew they were trying to run a game on me. For the first time since that morning, I allowed myself to relax a bit, knowing that I was no longer hapless. Now I was back in control of my destiny, setting a trap for any response that Dan might possibly give. I was confident that, on advice from company lawyers, he would not respond to my email. Under the circumstances, what could he say? A response or no response would put him between a rock and a hard place. We were on the record now, which would put me in a good position if there were any legal action down the road.

As I expected, Dan did not respond to my email. I had taken the first small step in a possibly long, long journey to fend off formidable foes, whom I did not intend to underestimate. But confident that I could outfox them, I could hear Marvin Gaye singing "Let's Get It On."

Dan had assured me that the dismantling of Community Relations would have no impact on my continuing as a Vice President of the company. He let me know that a new department was planned for me in the area of Consumer Affairs, which would focus on the Public Utilities Commission. Although my Community Relations staff of forty employees would soon be dismissed, I would be allowed to retain my assistant, Alline, and two other people of my choice.

I tried to get a more definitive answer about the job description for this position of Vice President of Consumer Affairs, but unfortunately I was unable to do so because Dan was always vague when I pressed him for information. In fact, the more I probed, the clearer it became that this was nothing more than an unsophisticated political assault on the Community Relations Department—and on me in particular. When the axe was just a few inches from my neck, I assembled all the people under me to inform them of the decision that had been made to dismantle Community Relations. Everyone was shocked and depressed. Not long after that, by the end of December 1997, a vibrant and effective department within the company vanished without a trace.

26

Officer Without Portfolio

I've always lived by this golden rule,
Whatever happens "don't blow your cool"
You've got to have nerves of steel
Never show folks what you honestly feel

—Oscar Brown, Jr.

For the next several months, every skill I had in my survival kit was tested. I wish I could say that I found the strength to handle this situation on my own, but I must admit that I relied heavily on the moral support and clear thinking of Glenda and my growing team of legal friends and advisors, including Johnnie Cochran, Willie Brown, and Gwen Moore, in addition to Elihu, John, and others.

The advice I received was essentially this: Stay cool. Don't do anything foolish. Ride it out. Under no circumstances was I to impulsively get angry and quit. My friends reminded me that I was a skilled lawyer, who had argued before the United States Supreme Court and won, and I could pursue external remedies if necessary, such as in the courts or the press, but I had the core skills to handle this internally. In fact, I could make this situation work to my advantage if I were patient and demonstrated my ability to show grace under fire.

The reasoning underlying the sage advice that I received was simple. There were only two possible outcomes: I would stay or I would go. If I stayed, the company would have to find a meaningful position for me as a VP. I would get clarification about the Consumer Affairs Department, or I would head another suitable department. If I left, it would be by my choice or their pushing. The officers who sought to force me out could initiate my termination by offering me a severance package, which would have to be handsome for me to accept it. If, on the other hand, I got angry and quit, I wouldn't receive the compensation—which likely would be sizable, given my roughly twenty-five-year tenure and record of success.

With Johnnie Cochran (my Kappa brother)

As I saw it, I would win whether I left or stayed. I knew how this would play out from a legal perspective if PG&E forced me out. My lawyer friends were prepared to make certain that if PG&E terminated my career, I would be delighted with the compensation. So, for the next eight months, an intriguing cat-and-mouse game was played.

I kept nagging Dan, who was now my boss, to define my new duties in Consumer Affairs, but no matter how hard I pressed him, I could never get a definitive answer. I even went so far as to develop a written charter for the new responsibilities, and submitted that to Dan, but he never responded. The officers who had concocted this whole scheme were clearly betting that I would eventually become frustrated and quit. But I had no intention of playing into their hands. Every time I met with Dan, I had a smile on my face. "I'm a team player," I would say, "and I'm willing to do whatever it takes to make this work."

I was playing the game!

The picture was this: there were four of us in my undefined department. Aside from me, there was my assistant, Alline; a Latina, Silvia Aldana, who dealt with state organizations; and an Asian gentleman, Timothy Leong, who dealt with national organizations. Even though technically the department no longer existed, I continued to hold the title of Vice President of Community Relations, and deployed the budget of our phantom department strategically. All of us understood exactly what was happening, but maintained a positive attitude as we developed a network of relationships across the country that would benefit the Consumer Affairs Department if PG&E ever formally established it and defined its objectives with clarity.

Since I had no clearly defined responsibilities, I could spend my time doing whatever I pleased, and I did just that, traveling across the nation to connect with all those organizations. Although I continued to report to Dan, my accountability was greatly reduced, which also diminished the level of my stress. As soon as I got back to my office after a meeting with him, I would send him an email, outlining the nature of our conversation, my suggestions, and, of course, my "loyal" commitment to making the new strategy succeed. In writing each email, I knew that I was, in fact, sending a message to the company lawyers. I'm certain that each time they read one of those emails, they must have had heartburn, because they realized there was little chance that I was going to resign. My former colleagues knew me as a crafty lawyer, which meant that if PG&E were to terminate me, the compensation was getting higher with each email.

In the late spring of 1998, Dick Clarke, my old mentor, who had been retired for three years, called me one day. He and I had stayed in touch, but I had never discussed my situation with him. Nevertheless, I could tell that he was aware of it. That conversation ended with him inviting me to lunch at the Boulevard, a popular downtown restaurant.

Almost from the moment we sat down, we talked about my predicament. Although he looked frail, his mind was sharp as he expressed outrage at what was being done to me. He was now an outsider, of course, but he let me know that he believed he still had some influence within the company, especially with the new President of PG&E, Gordon Smith, and he was going to use it to assist me. In the meantime, his advice was the same as that of my lawyer friends: Ride it out.

One unexpected but delightful development resulted from the game that PG&E was playing with me: I wound up with one of the most luxurious offices on the Executive Floor! How that happened is an interesting story.

During the time that the Community Relations Department was being dismantled, I learned that a decision had been made that all officers reporting to Dan, who was the Senior Vice President of Governmental Relations, would be moving to offices on the Executive Floor. Three years earlier, as Executive Assistant to President Stan Skinner, I had had a small office on that floor, a short distance from Stan's office, but that paled in comparison to the opulent wood-paneled offices enjoyed by senior officers. Where would they put me now?

Perhaps without thinking—which was unusual for Dan, who was an attorney—he stated in an email his desire to have his "team" together on the west side of the floor, but he expressly stated, "We should put Bob Harris on the other side."

What! Apparently, I was supposed to get angry and quit. Instead, I took advantage of Dan's indelicate statement to chide him for excluding me from his team. As I suspected, that put him on the defensive, and I enjoyed using my lawyer skills to have fun with him as he tried to explain what he had meant by his desire to have me on the other side.

"According to your email, Dan," I said, "I'm not a part of your team."

"That's not what I meant," he said, looking uncomfortable. "What I meant to say was that I wanted those officers with governmental relations responsibilities to be close to my office, and your responsibilities do not involve governmental relations."

Nevertheless, as far as I was concerned, his words spoke for themselves, and his defense was unsuccessful.

As I anticipated, I still landed on the east side of the floor, but I was assigned to an office that was better than anyone else's, presumably because it was the only one available on the "other side." The suite was truly elegant, with a great view of the bay and a three-room bathroom with a full shower—the only office on the Executive Floor so fully equipped! Fighting the war from the comfort of such elegant barracks certainly reduced the stress of daily battles.

Despite this opulence, Alline was furious with the company. She couldn't understand why I was continuing to do community relations activities when the department had been eliminated. I cautioned her to be patient, saying that I was not worried, so long as she and I were receiving our paychecks. She thought I was crazy for not letting PG&E have a piece of my mind, but I reminded her that my official title was still Vice President of Community Relations, and that as long as that was the case, I was going to continue to build relationships, while having lots of fun. Each time I assured her that there was an end game, which I intended to win.

While I did absolutely nothing to publicize my diminished role, rumors began to spread nevertheless. By late May of 1998, it had become obvious, both internally and externally, that I was an officer without portfolio. Many of the Black employees in the company were concerned, but understandably didn't raise any official objections. Nevertheless, they let their feelings be known informally through the grapevine. Numerous external associates, however, with whom I had built relationships over the years, began to inquire about what was going on with me at PG&E. For example, Eva J. Paterson, my friend of many years, who was a noted civil rights lawyer, called to express her dismay.

"I'd like to nail them to the cross!" she said.

"I'll call you if I need your help," I replied. "But I think I've got things under control."

A couple of weeks later, in late June, Gordon Smith, now President of PG&E, whose office was on the opposite end of the hall from me, came to my office with a puzzled look on his face, asking if he could chat with me.

Closing the door behind him, he said, "My office just got a call from the President of the San Francisco Branch of the NAACP, who requested to come see me."

Gordon seemed quite worried as he asked me whether I knew why. I told him I didn't know, but I suspected it was probably about me.

"Why would they want to see me about you?" he asked.

"I can call them for you. But, Gordon, they're probably concerned that the Community Relations Department has been dissolved, and that I'm an officer with a title but without a department."

With that, he said, "Let's go to my office and talk."

During the next hour in his office, I explained in detail everything that had happened over the past several months, laying all the facts on the table. He stood up, looked directly at me, and said, "Wow, you're an officer without portfolio, and that ain't right! I'm going to fix this."

I must admit that Gordon acted as if this matter were a complete surprise to him. I wondered about that, but I quickly concluded that it didn't matter. My focus was on what he was prepared to do.

As I left his office, I told him that I would call Alex Pitcher, the President of the San Francisco Branch of the NAACP, to actually find out why they wanted to see him, which I did when

I reached him the next day. After my conversation with Alex, whom I knew well, I wrote Gordon an email:

> I called Alex Pitcher to find out why they are coming to see you. He indicated that for several months they have been getting complaints about PG&E from PG&E employees, but didn't do anything in response. He then indicated that when he heard that I had been reduced to a "figurehead" and that the Company had turned its back on the Black community and was getting rid of Black employees, he decided to contact you personally.

To make certain that Gordon understood the gravity of the situation, I added:

> A number of Black leaders were especially upset about the perception that I was merely a "figurehead." I told him that you and I talked yesterday about future assignments, and I was confident that I will have a meaningful and appropriate officer assignment in the Company.

I noted, to underscore my rapport with the NAACP:

> I suggested that they not jump to any unwarranted conclusions about the Company and its commitment to the African American community. I told him that I thought he would find you to be a thoughtful and sincere CEO who is genuinely interested in excellent community relations.

Finally, I underscored what he should anticipate:

> I informed him that PG&E has been a longtime friend and supporter of the NAACP and values that relationship.

The email was intended to set the tone for the eventual meeting between Gordon and Alex. In particular, I wanted Gordon to know that this was a serious matter that required his leadership.

A few weeks later, before Gordon's meeting with representatives from the NAACP, I left for Memphis to attend the 1998 Annual Convention of the National Bar Association. A couple of days after my arrival, Alline called to tell me that Gordon wanted me to contact him, which I did immediately.

Sounding very enthusiastic, Gordon informed me that, for the past several months, the company had been working to establish an Environmental Affairs Department. That was a total surprise to me, but apparently Bains & Company, which PG&E had hired as a consultant, had been working quietly to lay out the details, which included recommendations for a Chief Environmental Officer to head the department. I listened intently as Gordon talked excitedly about creating the new department.

As I anticipated, he then stated that he would like me to become Vice President of the new department because he thought my credentials would make me ideal in that role, where I could position the company as an environmental leader in the industry. I quietly let him make his case, feeling that I had earned this moment of satisfaction.

Without hesitation, of course, I accepted his offer. Although I felt that the position had never been intended for me, thanks to the NAACP and other external forces, I would be getting it.

Gordon asked me to remain silent about this for the time being, but I would be joining the study team as its leader as soon as I got home.

When I returned, I learned that, while I was at the NBA conference, Gordon had met with Alex Pitcher and Toye Moses of the NAACP, who later told me what had happened.

The meeting was scheduled for 8:00 A.M., an hour when the Executive Floor was virtually empty. Gordon met them in person at the elevator and escorted them to his office, where he immediately began talking about me and what a valued officer I was. Then he explained that I had accepted a very important position at PG&E, which would be announced in a couple of months, as soon as the details of my new department were worked out. Finally, he walked them down the hall to my office, where he took great pride in showing them my elaborate bathroom, stressing that this was the only executive suite with a shower.

According to Alex and Toye, they were hardly able to get in a word during the entire visit, never once informing Gordon why they were there. He never bothered to ask, and personally escorted them back to the elevator.

As they left the building, they wondered why Gordon had placed such emphasis on my suite having the only shower. "Maybe," Toye said to Alex, "since the brother stinks, he needs to have a shower in his office." Later, we laughed again and again about what became known as the "shower tour." They never had to make a single verbal request. Their presence alone was demanding.

27

I've Won!

However long the night, the dawn will break.

—African Proverb

When I took over as leader of the study team, it was a clear indication to everyone that the person likely to head the new department was me. Nothing was announced officially, however, until two months later, after the team had concluded structuring the functions of the new department:

> SAN FRANCISCO — (BUSINESS WIRE) — Oct. 21, 1998 — In a move that deepens and renews Pacific Gas and Electric Company's longstanding commitment to the protection of the environment, the utility today announced the creation of the position of vice president of environmental affairs and has elected a veteran executive to head the department.
>
> Robert L. Harris, 54, currently vice president of community relations at Pacific Gas and Electric Company, will be responsible for all of the utility's environmental programs and initiatives, as well as assuring the highest compliance with all local, state,

and federal environmental laws and regulations.

"As we enter a new century, the stewardship of our natural resources will grow even more important," said Gordon Smith, president and chief executive officer of Pacific Gas and Electric Company.

As I began a new chapter in my career, I was singing with James Brown, "I Feel Good." For the next eight years, I remained on the Executive Floor, witnessing the departure of all those colleagues who had probably played a part in my becoming an officer without portfolio.

I served as Vice President of Environmental Affairs just as climate change was becoming a matter of serious public concern and debate. That was a good fit for this lawyer. As I managed a team of almost a hundred employees, I was responsible for environmental compliance in every aspect of the company's operations as it sought to be an environmental leader.

Of course, there were some challenges. One of the most visible ones came with the release of the movie *Erin Brockovich* in 2000, two years after I took over the new department. The film was based on a story involving PG&E, and let's just say it wasn't flattering to us. The story, set in Hinkley, California, a small town in the southern part of PG&E's territory, concerned our use of the chemical hexavalent chromium to clean corroded gas pipes. A number of the people in the town filed a lawsuit, claiming that the chemical was leaking into the water supply and causing cancer. In the end, the company settled the lawsuit for $333 million.

As the Vice President of Environmental Affairs, I was responsible for ensuring that PG&E not only complied with all environmental regulations, but also was perceived as an environmental leader. However, I didn't have to do much to maintain that perception, because PG&E had been an excellent environmental citizen for decades. In fact, from the millions of people who saw the movie, I received exactly *one* letter of complaint.

One of the projects I am proudest of was the closing of the Hunters Point Power Plant in San Francisco. Back in 1998, when I was the Vice President of Community Relations, health concerns attributed to the operation of the power plant began to be expressed by the predominantly African American residents of the area. Some people began blaming the power plant, which had been built in 1929, for the high levels of cancer and other diseases in the community, even though the recently closed Naval Shipyard in the neighborhood, which had many pollution issues, may have been more associated with those illnesses. However, since the shipyard was closed and the power plant was still operating, the natural assumption, although unproven, was that the illnesses were related to the plant.

The company executives had no real desire to close the plant, which they believed was essential to supplying energy to the Bay Area. As Vice President of Community Relations, I was responsible for calming the community. The local African American leaders were adamant that the plant be closed. The San Francisco Health Department concluded from its studies that (1) the residents were suffering from twice the average national rate of asthma; (2) cervical and breast cancers were occurring at noticeably higher rates than in the nation as a whole; and (3) a number of other illnesses had similarly alarming rates. Although none of this could be directly traced to the power plant, nevertheless environmental justice advocates began campaigning for PG&E to adhere to principles that required equal treatment of minority residents in environmentally impacted areas.

For me, this was a sensitive situation because of my civil rights background and my personal support of environmental justice principles. To make matters worse, PG&E was considering putting yet another power source in the area. The community and PG&E were definitely on a collision course.

As community activists began to consolidate their opposition to the power plant, when word spread about the potential additional power source, San Francisco's first Black mayor, Willie Brown, said, "The people of Bayview–Hunter's Point have been dumped on enough."

Clearly, the line was drawn in the sand. With Mayor Brown in opposition, it was obvious that the day of reckoning had come, and taking charge was the only escape route for me.

Although PG&E continued its official stance that the old plant was needed to meet the energy needs of the region, I began to meet with key community advocates to discuss with them the possibility of shutting it down. In fact, I injected myself into the power plant issue as forcefully as I could, enjoying entering the fray.

I was acutely aware of the community's position, and personally believed that the plant should be closed, but I knew that convincing the company would be difficult, to say the least. Sensing that there was a thinly disguised insensitivity to the plight of the community, I took every opportunity to argue that closure made good business sense.

In mid-July 1998, I was at a civic event also attended by Kofi Bonner, the Mayor's Economic Policy Advisor, who was a friend of mine, when the issue came up in our conversation. It didn't take us long to conclude that the best strategy for solving the problem was to get Mayor Brown to press PG&E into engaging in negotiations. In other words, we thought that with pressure from the mayor and with me pushing the company from the inside, we could get the parties to sit down and discuss the issue seriously.

Receiving the Father of the Year Award

Not surprisingly, additional pressure was necessary. The impasse shifted considerably when Bonner astutely threatened PG&E by indicating that the city was prepared to institute imminent domain proceedings, taking ownership of the property and closing the plant.

The threat worked, and after extended discussions between PG&E and the mayor's office, a decision was finally made to close the plant—a move that was hailed by the community as a tremendous victory.

The media had long been following the controversy. An article published in the *San Francisco Chronicle* on July 18, 1998, reported: "In a stunning turn of events, Pacific Gas and Electric Co. agreed yesterday to shut down its controversial Hunters Point power plant, rather than continue fighting the city's hardball efforts."

Thus, the initial step for closing the plant had been taken. However, city, state, and federal regulations had to be followed, which took another eight years before the plant was shut down.

As fate would have it, three months after the decision was made to close the plant, I was appointed Vice President of Environmental Affairs, so it was my responsibility to take charge of the process that led to the final closure in May 2006. That was a personal victory for me—my last, long, hard-fought battle at PG&E.

At the formal closing ceremony, the president of the A. Philip Randolph Institute, James Bryant, who had become a close ally of mine during the eight-year closing process, observed, "I want to respect the fact that PG&E has kept its word." That meant everything to me.

With Members of the Sigma Pi Phi Fraternity (The Boulé)

That year, 2006, was momentous for me in others way as well. For one, I became Grand Sire Archon-Elect (national president in waiting) of Sigma Pi Phi Fraternity, informally known as the Boulé. Founded in 1904 in Philadelphia, the fraternity's members include African American men of high achievement, with approximately 5,000 members nationally and in the Bahamas and England. This by-invitation-only fraternity includes senior executives of leading corporations and national leaders in law, politics, business, medicine, education, and many other fields and professions.

Celebrating My Retirement

That year I also retired. My last day at the office was November 30, 2006. When I handed my office key to Alline and left the Executive Floor, it was with a sense of accomplishment and excitement. I had no regrets. Having weathered many storms while winning many battles, I felt a sense of joy that, at the age of 62, I had accomplished what few other officers had achieved in recent years. I was leaving at full retirement age on my own terms rather than being asked to leave, which was the norm. As I walked out onto Market Street, I could hear Frank Sinatra singing, "I Did It My Way."

Over 400 people attended my retirement celebration at the Oakland Airport Hilton Ballroom. Robert Duckworth, a comedian and Kappa Alpha Psi brother of mine, joked that my retirement party was the first he had ever heard of that was sold out. Scalpers, he said, were selling tickets up and down the street outside, with people offering to pay outrageous prices to get in! What stands out in my mind is the number of friends who came from across the country, as well as the huge local turnout, including many people from PG&E. I was so grateful.

28

Looking Back... and Forth

I've known rivers:
I've known rivers ancient as the world
    and older than the flow of human blood in
    human veins.
My soul has grown deep like the rivers.

                    —Langston Hughes

My final words in this book are directed primarily at young African American professionals in the corporate world and those men and women who aspire to be there. I have met and currently mentor some truly outstanding young professionals, who are the foundation of our future.

My first job as a lawyer at PG&E led to a remarkable 34-year career. I could never have foreseen that when I was a child picking cotton in rural Arkansas. Nor when I was a teenager on a Continental Trailways bus, leaving my beloved parents behind in Arkadelphia. Nor when I was a student doing domestic work in Oakland, determined to be the first in my immediate family to graduate from college. Nor when I was given the opportunity to attend one of the most prestigious law schools in the country. I have been blessed.

One of the keys to my success was a vast network of friends across the country. You never know what fate has in store for you, but you are surely better equipped to deal with challenges if you have supportive, wise friends.

When I began my tenure at PG&E in 1972, I decided from the start that it would be important for me to have friends both inside and outside the company. As I have described in other chapters, I made it a point to meet early on with nearly every Black professional at PG&E. We lunched together and sometimes gathered during work breaks or after work to talk about the obstacles we faced in our various departments.

I am especially grateful for having had in my first boss, Dick Clarke, a valuable mentor, who later became PG&E's Chairman and CEO. Dick got me off on the right foot, encouraged and supported me, and saw to it that I was given opportunities to grow. There were other allies as well, but none as influential as Dick.

With President Bill Clinton and Congresswoman Barbara Lee

What helped me more than anything else, in terms of navigating the turbulent waters at PG&E, was the support network I built outside the company. Whatever was happening to me within the organization, at each stage I was able to contact people like Elihu Harris, John Burris, Eva Patterson, Gwen Moore, Johnnie Cochran, Willie Brown, Ben Travis, and many others who were willing to give their counsel and assistance.

Failure to recognize the importance of friendships and to correctly read the cues from individuals who are not in your corner can rapidly derail your career. Remember, it is not rattlesnakes that threaten you, but your lack of awareness of their presence that can prove deadly.

You can never forget that you are Black, and that you will sometimes be treated differently solely because of that. It is unwise to forget the history of race relations in America. First, we were slaves. Then we were barely paid workers, like sharecroppers who could never get out of debt. Next, we were excluded from unions and forced to serve in menial positions in the military. Then came equal opportunity in employment, a radical new concept. But while laws can change behavior, they can't change attitudes.

If you trust others whom you believe have your best interests at heart, you may learn that you are sometimes wrong. Allies in corporate settings may not always have your best interests at heart. They have their own agendas and will sometimes be willing to do whatever is necessary to advance themselves, even at your expense. Recognizing that risk will enhance your ability to survive. Smile when they smile, but remember the lyrics of the song "Back Stabbers" by the O'Jays, which climbed to the top of the charts in 1972:

They smile in your face
All the time they want to take your place
The back stabbers
Back stabbers

There's nothing wrong with trusting others. You should. But never trust without verifying that you have placed that trust wisely. If your trust is not well placed, then it can become deadly. You needn't walk around constantly looking over your shoulder, expecting someone to stab you in the back. However, you need to be careful.

The late Dr. Walter Shervington, a Black psychiatrist and a friend of mine, who served as President of the National Medical Association, said, "It's mentally healthy for Blacks in America to be a little paranoid, given our racist history."

That is unfortunately a lesson that I see some young Blacks *not* learning as they try to navigate the waters of Corporate America. Thinking that it's a new, fairer day, they don't protect themselves and eventually are derailed when they are confronted with racism in the workplace.

I recall a smart, attractive, young African American lawyer, who came to PG&E's legal department in the early 1980s. From the very beginning, she associated almost exclusively with white lawyers and had very little inclination to develop relationships with me or the two other Black lawyers in the department at that time. Although she apparently thought I was unessential to her career, she would occasionally stop by my office to say hello.

When I shared my experiences with her about surviving in the legal department, she would say, after listening politely:

"I'm different from you. Don't worry about me." Nevertheless, I encouraged her to join the Charles Houston Bar Association, but she declined.

After a while, word began to spread that she was spending most of her evening hours drinking with some of the white male lawyers. I let her know what people were saying, but she insisted that it was none of my business. But within a year of her arrival at PG&E, she was gone, primarily because she had failed to see that certain behaviors are what I call "career derailers."

There is nothing wrong per se with associating with colleagues after work, but you need to know the pitfalls and how to avoid them. People will talk, and not all the stories they tell will be true or fair. Once you get a bad reputation, it's almost impossible to get rid of it. The key is to assume that every moment of your life is being viewed by a camera, so you should ask yourself if your behavior would be appropriate for the front page of the daily newspaper.

The young lady's quiet exit illustrates the importance of being judicious in whatever social relations you establish in the workplace. Everything a Black employee does is under scrutiny, and any deviations that appear to indicate that you are engaging in inappropriate relationships will weigh heavily against you, even though a white colleague may engage in identical behavior without repercussions.

I also recall a Black man with Ivy League credentials for college and law school who came into PG&E with the same unfortunate strategy of colorblind networking. He did very well for a number of years, perhaps as long as a decade, and was ultimately promoted to supervise a unit outside the legal department. Although he had a good relationship with me, he did not have a cadre of external advisors in the Black professional community outside of PG&E.

After a while, he began to experience unusual difficulties in supervising his all-white unit of non-lawyers handling rate cases, and encountered conspiracies and attempts to derail him. When that happened, his reaction was one of utter dismay. When he and I chatted extensively about his predicament, it was clear to me that he had never learned the importance of developing both internal and external relationships—in particular, relationships with friends and mentors in whom he could confide.

One day as we sat in my office talking, he was nearly in tears, since he couldn't understand what was going on or why. I spent considerable time trying to explain to him that he unaware of his environment. As I said before, when you are not aware of the rattlesnakes surrounding you, you are likely to get bitten. Soon after that, he left to join another company— where he took that valuable lesson with him.

Each generation makes its own contribution to society in a different way. If you believe many history books, William Lloyd Garrison, a White man, led the abolitionist movement in the nineteenth century. Actually, Frederick Douglass, a runaway slave, orator, writer, and newspaper publisher par excellence ought to get as much credit or more. "If there is no struggle," he famously said, "there is no progress." Douglass was a lifelong warrior, who sat down with not one but two presidents at the White House to negotiate the terms of emancipation.

In the early twentieth century, in the face of lynchings

and Jim Crow laws, the NAACP was founded in 1909. Then came the Great Migration, during which Black folks from the segregated South travelled in search of better lives in the North and West, where they were met with housing and employment discrimination. During the 1950s and 1960s, the battle continued with the modern civil rights movement, which attracted thousands of participants. With the success of that movement, the dynamics of race in this country were changed; but during that transition, many people were whipped, jailed, and even killed, including the movement's most prominent leader, Dr. Martin Luther King, Jr.

With My Siblings: Charles, Harold, Jean, & Leonard

My own generation, consisting of people who grew up in the 1960s and 1970s, witnessed—and in many cases, participated in—the struggle or found ways to support it. Many of them, however, are now expressing disappointment and frustration with the generation coming of age right now, the so-called millennials. These young folks, the argument goes, seem less committed than their elders to causes, to advocacy, to helping others, and to taking political stands. While I have seen some millennials step up, far too many seem politically apathetic, lacking an understanding of the tremendous sacrifices that led to the lives and careers they are enjoying today.

Although this current generation has benefitted greatly from the committed efforts of prior generations, many of its members seem to take little action to improve the lives of others in the Black community who do not share their prosperity. In particular, Black members of the legal profession should be encouraged to devote time to pro bono work. When I see lawyers not incorporating civil rights advocacy into their careers, I am pained, because I know what the Black lawyers of my own generation and the generations before me accomplished on behalf of the Black community. To many young Black lawyers, I have repeated the words of Charles Hamilton Houston: "A lawyer is either a social engineer or a parasite on society."

But it's not just lawyers we need. Members of all professions have talents that can contribute to help lift up the Black community. These individuals have status and skills, yet many of them are only concerned with self-aggrandizement and self-indulgence. I place some of the blame for that on members of my own generation. Perhaps we painted a picture that focused on how far we have come, suggesting that the battle for equality is over, so there's not much more to accomplish in the area of civil rights.

Perhaps we didn't spend enough time talking about Maria Stewart, Frederick Douglass, Harriet Tubman, Harriet Jacobs, Ida B. Wells, W. E. B. Du Bois, Booker T. Washington, Marcus Garvey, Mary McCloud Bethune, A. Philip Randolph, Charles

Hamilton Houston, Thurgood Marshall, Martin Luther King, Jr., Fannie Lou Hamer, Malcolm X, and all the other heroes and heroines who have advocated for us. Other cultures ensure that their history is passed down from generation to generation. The Holocaust, for instance, will never be diminished in the minds of Jews.

Today, some Americans, mostly Whites, argue that we live in a post-racial society, pointing to the fact that America elected a Black President. But look at the backlash—the seething racism that Barack Obama's election unleashed: the birther movement spearheaded by Donald Trump, the Tea Party, and the unprecedented incivility displayed by congressional and other Republicans toward the President. The Republicans say they want to "Take Back Our Country." From whom? After eight years of a Black President, Trump wants to "Make America Great Again"—without mentioning when it *stopped* being great.

With voter I.D. laws and other similarly cynical measures, some of the gains of the civil rights struggle could be in jeopardy. It has happened before, such as during Reconstruction, and that's just one reason why Black millennials must know their history, so they'll understand exactly what's at stake. Although a Black man was elected President, we must remember that *only* 43 percent of Whites voted for him in 2008, which dropped to 39 percent in 2012.

History, let's not forget, has a way of repeating itself. If you don't know what happened during Reconstruction, google it, buy a book, or borrow one from the library. It's never too late to learn.

Social activism has always been an essential part of my

career. Beginning in the 1970s, as I was leading the Charles Houston Bar Association, I was heavily involved in taking on the police for the shooting of young Black males. I continued to focus on that issue when I became President of the National Bar Association. Thus, I was part of the "Black Lives Matter" campaign long before the slogan was adopted by our current generation of young activists. In other words, for me, this is a renewal of an old issue that continues to permeate Black communities.

With Charles and Jean

When I look back now to review the course of my career, I recall how extraordinarily happy I was to get out of rural Arkansas, as if moving to California in 1960 were a guaranteed path to success. It was not. What really led to my successful career were the lessons I took with me from across the Ouachita River in rural Manchester. Without question, those lessons guided the choices I made as an adult.

For instance, how did I learn the importance of developing

a network of Black professional friends as a young lawyer? The truth is, no one had to teach me that when I came to California. I already knew it back in Arkansas—as did any Black person who grew up in a place and time when racial segregation was legal. Back then, I didn't play with White children, or go to school with them, or eat with them, or share libraries, public parks, public toilets, or water fountains. As a result, Black folks had to depend on each other. We didn't go to the police to settle our disputes or kill each other over clothing.

We found other ways to resolve our conflicts by ourselves. We couldn't go to a bank for a loan to finance a car purchase or a home, so we had to save and lend to each other, which made for stronger families and stronger communities.

The Harris Family, with Glenda's Mother Behind the Couch

When I entered the corporate world, I knew I needed my community's support. I also knew the importance of confidence. Marcus Garvey put it best: "If you have no confidence in self, you are twice defeated in the race of life. With confidence you have won even before you have started."

Booker T. Washington, the founder of Tuskegee Institute, who began life as a slave, observed: "Success is to be measured not so much by the position that one has reached in life as by the obstacles which he has overcome while trying to succeed." My own success, I think, had a lot to do with the way I viewed "obstacles." Some people see them as impediments; I've always seen them as opportunities. Where did I get that worldview? From my family, of course.

Everything we owned in our small tin-roofed home, we had to create ourselves. We literally had to exploit every resource we had in order to produce the food, clothing, and shelter we needed. And we couldn't waste a thing. If something could have a useful new life as something else, it got it. We converted, adapted, redeveloped, and recycled everything in sight. Before discarding something, my first thought always was, *Can I do something with this?* So, everything was a potential opportunity. Later, I carried that creative determination into adulthood. As I have said several times before in this memoir, a setback was something I always tried to see as a setup for a comeback.

Finally, I want to leave you with a quote from Frederick Douglass: "People might not get all they work for, but they must certainly work for all they get." That's true whether you are picking cotton and your pay is determined by the weight of your labor, or you are arguing a case before the United States Supreme Court and your success is determined by the weight of your arguments.

So, work hard!

Index

Social activism as part of career,
  295–296
Socratic Method, practicing of, 114–115
Socratic questioning, as a learning tool,
  115
Stanford Law School, 205
Sudduth, Charles "Jack", 88, 102

T

Ten Commandments, 30
The Commons, 86
Time management, 138
Travis, Benjamin, attorney, 156, 181
TURN (Toward Utility Rate Normaliza-
  tion), 197

U

UC Berkeley's law school, 83, 103, 108,
  133
U.S. Supreme Court
  annual review of cases, 216
  Brown v. Board of Education, decision
    on, 48
  First National Bank of Boston vs.
    Bellotti, 435 U.S. 765, 213
  juveniles subject to same standard of
    proof as adults, 101
  Newman, Theodore R. Jr., 210–211
  PG&E case against CPUC's decision,
    204–216

V

Voting Rights Act of 1965, 98

W

Western Province convention, 1973, San
  Jose, 165
  delegate votes secured before
    elections, 165–166
  Grand Polemarch, elected as, 170
  Grand Polemarch, elections for,
    166–170

White folks, 13
"Whites Only, "11
Williams Elementary School, 7, 40–42,
  52
  1949, earliest memory of, 41–42
  Braggs, S.A., 43–47
  College, Evelyn (Miss), 43
  disruption, consequences of, 43
  educational tools, 42
  enrolled in the first grade, 41–42
  graduation from, 47
  no fear of transitioning to fifth grade,
    46
  swift punishment, certainty of, 43
Williams, Flossie, 28
Williams, Mary, 6
Williams, Tom, 90–91
Work conditions, 14–15
Writing legal documents, 109